MYSTERIES
of the
TAYOS CAVES

"*Mysteries of the Tayos Caves* is an utterly fascinating book that delves into the amazing history, legends, stories, and traditions of the vast Tayos cave system in the Amazon and the spectacular treasures and earth-shattering secrets said to be hidden there. This book also chronicles the author's own harrowing exploration of the cave system. From beginning to end, a gripping read!"

DOUGLAS PRESTON, AUTHOR OF
THE LOST CITY OF THE MONKEY GOD

"As a person who has spent decades looking for a legend, I can appreciate Alex's tenacity about the mystery of the Tayos. Alex leaves no stone unturned and explores every crevice of the Tayos story."

STEVE ELKINS,
AMERICAN CINEMATOGRAPHER AND EXPLORER

MYSTERIES

of the

TAYOS CAVES

*The Lost Civilizations Where the
Andes Meet the Amazon*

ALEX CHIONETTI

Bear & Company
Rochester, Vermont

Bear & Company
One Park Street
Rochester, Vermont 05767
www.BearandCompanyBooks.com

Text stock is SFI certified

Bear & Company is a division of Inner Traditions International

Cataloging-in-Publication Data for this title is available from the Library of Congress

ISBN 978-1-59143-356-9 (print)
ISBN 978-1-59143-357-6 (ebook)

Printed and bound in the United States by Lake Book Manufacturing, Inc. The text stock is SFI certified. The Sustainable Forestry Initiative® program promotes sustainable forest management.

10 9 8 7 6 5 4 3 2 1

Text design and layout by Debbie Glogover
This book was typeset in Garamond Premier Pro with Nocturne Serif, ITC Legacy Sans Std, and Gill Sans MT Pro used as display fonts

To send correspondence to the author of this book, mail a first-class letter to the author c/o Inner Traditions • Bear & Company, One Park Street, Rochester, VT 05767, and we will forward the communication.

Contents

APPENDICES

Acknowledgments

I would like to first thank the widow of Petronio Jaramillo Abarca; Xavier Alvarado; Mathias Spatz; Gerardo Peña Matheus; Carlos Peña Matheus; Roberto Perujo; Eduardo Mahuat; Mario Sánchez; and Omar Guevara for their help and understanding in my search, and for the support they gave me during my first expedition in Ecuador.

In Argentina, I would like to thank Micaela Goyén Aguado for all those years of communication and for the access she gave me to Juan Moricz's materials in Buenos Aires.

Furthermore, I am grateful for the long, kind, and polemical conversations I had with Guillermo Aguirre and Debora Goldstern, on the phone and in person in Buenos Aires, before and after my expeditions.

A special mention for Javier Stagnaro; our friendship with Julio Goyén Aguado brought us close through the decades. And to Antonio "Tono" Huneeus for the recent finding and for our age-old connection to Ecuador and to the South American Andes.

I would like to thank the late Andrés Fernández Salvador Zaldumbide; Héctor Polit; Stanley Hall's widow, Elaine Hall; Jorge Salvador Lara; the late Hernán Crespo; the late Gastón Fernández Borrero; the Sharupi family; Lucho Nivelo; Stan Grist; Jaime Rodriguez; the late Héctor Burgos Stone; Horacio Spotorno; the late Lilian Icaza; and Monica Williams.

I would also like to thank my wife at that particular time, Patricia, who was praying in my favorite spot at Saint James Parish, in Red Bank, New Jersey, before a beautiful and sober-looking statue of the Virgin Mary by a nineteenth-century Italian sculptor (she is shown treading on a snake with her left foot), right at the moment we were surrounded by a gang of renegade Shuars who came for our heads.

May We Not Be Ashamed of the Future

Half a century ago, while the world was concentrating on its television screens to see the arrival of the first man on the moon, in an office in the Ecuadorian city of Guayaquil, there was a scene from another world. On that July 21, 1969, an Argentine citizen of Hungarian origin named Janos "Juan" Moricz made public a testimony that revealed him to be the discoverer of a network of artificial tunnels, created by an unknown civilization, that lay under a good part of Ecuador. That document can be read on page 55 of this book.

That notarized document not only referred to a colossal infrastructure hitherto unpublished in the so-called civilized world, but also mentioned a collection—a library, rather—of metal and gold plates whose knowledge and exotic motifs represented the culture of its builders. From his testimony it was clear that Moricz did not seek ownership of that treasure but only recognition—and protection—of what he considered a finding "of unimaginable cultural value."

The unstable political situation of Ecuador in those years left Moricz's pleas for preservation unheard. A man of an overwhelming personality, of a fiery and impatient nature, Moricz despaired at the inaction of the authorities. As the weeks went by, he retired into business and left the matter in the hands of his lawyer, Gerardo Peña Matheus. It was through him that Erich von Däniken—the celebrated author of *Chariots of the Gods* (1968)—contacted Moricz. Von Däniken reconstructed Moricz's history; met with collateral witnesses such as the Salesian priest Carlo Crespi, who had been receiving bronze and gold plates from the natives of Cuenca for years as those of the caves; and wrote a book that would turn Moricz's discovery into something of world interest: *The Gold of the Gods* (1972).

Incredible as it may seem, in September 2018 the embers of this affair were still hot. The idea that these plates formed a kind of lost library of humanity, in which it was not difficult to find remote representations of Egyptian and even Phoenician or Babylonian origin, was still the subject of debate in publications, congresses, and social networks. What people, when and for what purpose, made those engraved plates and hid them in the equatorial depths? In the end, no one really knows.

Moricz seemed capable of providing a sensible response. He spoke of the Taltos, a Hungarian term to refer to some mysterious superior beings that created our species. He even suggested that their writing resembled the Magyar of his native land. Others, however, began to talk about intraterrestrials. In the absence of government explorations, most eventually ignored the issue.

In a personal effort to reconstruct what happened five decades ago, I visited Cuenca, Ecuador. Of the collection of Father Crespi there was no longer any trace. I interviewed journalists from the newspaper *El Comercio* and some interested writers and managed to meet with the only living witness of the dilemma that still remained alive in Guayaquil: the lawyer Don Gerardo Peña Matheus.

Peña Matheus was a gentleman, just as he has been portrayed by those who write about the mysteries of the caves. The literate octogenarian picked me up in the lobby of the Wyndhall Hotel, where I was staying, and sat at his desk to explain in detail what happened in the sixties. In the heat of some whiskeys, we remembered Moricz, who died in February 1991. He told me about Moricz's passion for archaeology and old books, and he confirmed the frustration that Moricz took to the grave for failing to turn his find into something of official importance. "The natives of the region where he found the galleries commissioned him to protect the legacy they showed him," he told me. "For them, those galleries were a heritage of their remote ancestors. A treasure to protect."

Peña Matheus and his charming wife, Mariana, did not let me doubt for a moment that a treasure is still hidden underground beneath Ecuador. Listening to them rekindled my memory of other adventurers who later wanted to emulate Moricz' steps, such as Andreas Faber-Kaiser or Alex Chionetti. Faber-Kaiser visited the region in the eighties, alone, without speleological equipment or the training to achieve his purpose. Before his death in 1994, Faber-Kaiser told me that he trusted that he would be initiated by the Shuar community—which to this day guards the main entrance to that network of tunnels—and perhaps that they would lead him to the "metal library" that the caves shelter. He did not get the initiation he had hoped for. The Shuar only allowed him to approach the mouth of the entrance—a vertical chasm of more than 200 feet of free fall—with the warning that he should be very careful to hold his tongue.

"Janos and I warned him that he might not get out of the Shuar territory alive," Peña Matheus told me, his eyes burning with passion.

That look, by the way, was the same that I had seen years before in the face of Alex Chionetti when he told me again and again of his own determination to vindicate the history and discovery of Moricz. Chionetti has dedicated almost four decades to this endeavor. He has traveled half the world looking for the threads of this hiding place, and he has interviewed the protagonists and drawn his own conclusions. But above all, his quest has been armed with courage and determination to explore, measure, and even film that underground world in Ecuador that today experts know as the Cuevas de los Tayos—the Tayos Caves.

I remember that while I was director of the important Spanish monthly magazine *Más Allá de la Ciencia* (Beyond science), Alex tried to persuade me several times to do a thorough follow-up on the subject. I only half listened, and now I regret it. After my recent encounter with Peña Matheus in Guayaquil, the efforts of some journalists, including mine, to locate the Crespi collection, and my conversations with modern local scholars such as Manuel Palacios, I have no doubt now that we are dealing with a topic of importance. The controversy that surrounds these caves is the logical consequence of a full-fledged archaeological enigma, perhaps the last of the great mysteries whose origins remain to be discovered.

From my point of view, it matters little whether it was a controversial author such as von Däniken who linked the galleries to an extraterrestrial civilization and who made the caves a public issue, or that the authorities of Ecuador continue to turn their back on what was discovered by Moricz and protected by Crespi. The case is still there, open to the eyes of the world. Alex Chionetti's endeavors, like those of a flesh-and-blood Indiana Jones, serve as reminders to us. Hopefully our generation does not have to be ashamed before our children and grandchildren for not managing a heritage such as the one that this book claims.

Final note: History is almost always capricious. Neil Armstrong—the man who, on July 21, 1969, was taking his first steps on the moon while Janos Moricz signed his famous testimony—came to visit the Caves of Tayos on a predestined day in July 1976. The story of Neil Armstrong is another great lesson hidden in this work. Look for it and enjoy it.

JAVIER SIERRA
MADRID, 2019

Award-winning author and journalist JAVIER SIERRA has contributed to a wide range of print publications and nonprint media venues. In 1990, he cofounded the monthly magazine *Año Cero* (Year zero). He was also the director of the magazine *Más Allá de la Ciencia* (Beyond science) for seven years, as well as a participant in several radio and television programs. Today, he focuses his effort researching and writing historical nonfiction and novels about ancient mysteries. His book *The Secret Supper* was a New York Times best seller. His other best-known works include *The Lost Angel, The Lady in Blue,* and *The Master of the Prado.* Sierra's work has been published in forty languages. Because he is a resident of Madrid, the Public Library of the State of Teruel can be consulted for information about Spanish and world editions of his work.

To Believe or
Not to Believe

What lies behind the word *tayos*? *Tayos* are nocturnal birds long known by indigenous populations of South America for their many practical uses. The birds dwell in caves, and their name has been given to the caves of Peru and Ecuador that they populate. They are also known as *oilbirds* or *aves guaneras*. Since

The author of this book holding a tayo bird

they are blind, they use sonar for flying inside or outside the caves that are their home. These caves are more than just mysterious caverns hidden deep in the Amazon jungle. In only half a century, countless enigmas have surfaced around them, all told by bizarre characters that could be described as crazy, holy, intrepid, or pathological criminals.

Are their stories all true, or are they a plethora of lies? Are the stories of the explorations of the Oilbird or Tayos Caves one of the biggest archaeological frauds or one of the greatest stories ever told?

The stories told about the Tayos Caves rely on the narratives of individuals rather than on hard evidence. The stories hold that all manner of objects have been spotted in the caves—golden plates, a metallic library, statues, a crystal and gold skeleton, ashlars of reddish stone colored with stony inscriptions, and petroglyphs of a hieroglyphic nature. A recent finding on one of the walls could be a natural formation, but it looks similar to Phoenician symbols. Perhaps it is nature imitating traces of a lost humanity.

This story of the Tayos Caves is a self-perpetuating story, maybe because through the years those of us who are involved have been witnesses of the original narrative, because we didn't want to be let down, because we wanted to know, to come close. To find the truth has been a part of each of our lives. A half-truth, a lie believed even by those who have told it over and over again. Every legend can originate from real facts, and this is something I have come to believe, as an explorer, in the last decade. In the midst of all this, it might just be the story of the people who live within the illusion of the mist that covers the pale green tops of the jungle trees.

Throughout these years, I became one of those characters, a desperate explorer who tried to continue what my colleagues could not finish; some of them became friends, others competitors, and some even enemies. I was an explorer who was going to have to face possible death for believing in his dreams and in the nightmares of others. At one point, I started to wonder who had lied, why I had let them lie to me, and why I lied to myself for so long.

For years I was a blind believer, but then I witnessed it with my own eyes, and I couldn't believe what I had once believed. Being there was proof of what could be, but also irrevocable evidence of what could *not* be. Things were not black-and-white, but they weren't gray either. I could see what I was looking for in an altered state of awareness.

The story had been deformed by those of us investigating it. I remember I asked Robert Ballard, who discovered the *Titanic*, if he thought a person observing too much, or concentrating on a particular object of study for too long, could modify the observed object. He answered, with a straight face, that yes, it was very possible.

This is what has happened with the Tayos Caverns: the story has focused on only two points, which are in the periphery, but not on the other places that could have been or that could be.

But what is the magic around the Tayos Caves? What is the fatal curiosity bug, the mortal hook that has lured certain individuals to try to find what apparently doesn't exist? A sort of chimera? A new El Dorado? What lies behind this force, this allure, this desire to find the treasure of the Tayos Caves? If we can even call it *treasure,* if it actually exists as such.

What is the physical and metaphysical force that has pulled some of us, whether we are a part of "the circle of the Tayos" or not, to stand firm and try to unravel such a tortuous and disregarded topic that seems to be a scam, a lie, or an illusion that we do not dare challenge, because we cannot answer it.

This book has taken more than thirty years of my life, years of searching, waiting, and hoping.

The obsession with solving the great mystery of the Tayos has been compared to that of the Marcahuasi Ruins, another site in the Peruvian Andes of archaeological, anthropological, and human interest that has kept me awake for many nights throughout my life. There is no doubt that the two places are connected by a number of elements and forms, as I could see for myself, and as others before me had confirmed when they ventured into these places.

During these decades, the time invested has been the best way to measure these countless secrets. They have multiplied largely because of the very passing of time, which sometimes enhances mysteries, especially those of an archetypal nature. Time is the best judge and executioner for every truth, for every half lie.

People asked me, and still ask, why, after so long, I risked everything to get to the Tayos Caves, and I sometimes answer with a little humor, paraphrasing mountaineer colleagues who climb Everest: because it has been there for a long, long time, and no one has dared go back to discover it. The Tayos Caves are like the Everest of speleology and sacred sites.

Fortunately or not, several individuals, who were characters in every sense of the word, came before me. If I had to reconstruct the story without their experiences, it would not exist, or it would be completely different. One thing is true: the Tayos Caves, aside from being a speleological wonder, have archaeological and architectonic shapes within them. These artifacts are found not only in this cavern, but also in other caves of the Tayos system located in several rivers that flow to the deltas of the Morona-Santiago and Pastaza provinces.

The official discovery of the caves is generally credited to Janos "Juan" Moricz, whose testimony regarding his discovery can be read on page 55. Following his announcement, Petronio Jaramillo Abarca would recount his experience exploring the caves as a young boy. The Scottish explorer Stanley Hall would get involved in explorations in the 1970s (and would famously invite astronaut Neil Armstrong to the caves), Erich von Däniken would publish a book about the caves in 1972, and Andreas Faber-Kaiser would try his luck in the 1980s.

I would come onto the scene in the 1980s, and I have been exploring Ecuador and Peru ever since. My first visits to the alleged Tayos Caves occurred in the early 2000s.

The main story behind the golden plates is connected to what we know (and don't know) of the Father Crespi Museum. My hypothesis is that all the plates attributed to the Tayos actually come from the Azuay and Cañar Provinces. This will remain my theory until a more in-depth analysis of the plates is made.

I don't know if I have solved the mystery, but the good news is that the millennia-old enigma of the Tayos is still alive, untouched, and hidden within us as an archetype in the darkest and clearest parts of our hearts and minds. In the end, human beings are still the last and greatest mystery. They are the measure of all things, and they can be seen documented in the millennia-old ceramics and artistic records of extinct tribes or civilizations.

I have to give thanks to the people who helped me as I took that long and remote path through the Amazon jungle and the northern Andes. I especially have to thank the shaman of La Esperanza, "Lucho" Chamin. He was in a dream I had the night before I started that last crusade into the caves. I saw him as a child innocently asking me to take him to see the birds in the cave. Without his unconditional support and his belief in the access permits granted to me by the Shuar authorities—after a bureaucratic hell of rejections that took five months of waiting and hopelessness, capping three decades of unbelievable delays—my dream would have never been fulfilled.

A second, "Masma" dream had been keeping me up at night since the late 1970s, when I came across an ancient advanced civilization that might have come from the stars. Why "Masma"? Daniel Ruzo, one of my teachers, and also a great influence and inspiration for me, coined this word to express the mystery of the advanced builders who left their colossal works on the highest peaks and under the Earth's surface.

Solving this mystery was my first objective. The second one was finding the metallic library, something I had always believed existed, thanks to my friendship with one of the first figures in the discovery of the caves. Tangential evidence was there for everyone to see in my notebooks and camera recordings before the astonished eyes of my expedition colleagues. We had gone down and come back out with some minor bruises and scratches, and we survived many threats and attempts against our lives after we left the sacred caves.

All this and more is in the past and will not happen again. Other explorers will come and go, but I will still wonder about the "treasure," at least in its physical form. I wonder if it will ever be found, if all these years of searching could help other explorers who will follow me, or who are brave enough to enter the circles of hell that this topic can be.

I don't know if there is still something down there, as Erich von Däniken still believes and claims (maybe to atone for guilt for an unethical past that can't be changed and has started to be revealed). If we talk about morals in regard to exploration, it is clear that the one who has a claim to the discovery is the person who gets there first, or who achieves something unprecedented by recording what others have not been able to do before him. Maybe if we continue looking with innocent eyes, similar to those of the Little Prince of Antoine de Saint-Exupéry, lost in the desert—or jungle—of the soul, we might be able to discern them and get a glimpse of them at the time of our sacred death.

Maybe the mystery is not what we think, and we don't deserve to unravel it in these changing times, or maybe it disappeared before our eyes without our even realizing it.

However, there is no doubt that the Tayos Caves have been, and will continue being, a challenge for those who remember, or at least for those with a spirit thirsty for knowledge and for solving our planet's mysteries. To believe or not to believe—that is the question.

1

Green Labyrinth

Ecuador was and is the center of the planet, and it has been the cultural center of our planet since uncharted times.

The Tayos Caves are, without a doubt, one of the most complex mysteries an archaeological detective could come upon. Some will see them from a pragmatic angle, others from a mystical one, and others from an almost fanatically subjective point of view.

Unfortunately, many of the main witnesses have already left us, and they have taken their truths and their lies with them. Those of us who remain are the ones who learned about the story directly from some of those who set the stage, and from others who have gotten on that same stage with passion in order to defeat boredom and find meaning in their lives.

The Tayos represent many things. They are Ecuador at its finest; they are its essence, its impenetrable jungles, and the mystery of more than one race but especially the indigenous people known as the Jíbaros or Shuar. They are the sum of the archetypes that take us back to a South America that was reinterpreted from the outside, only to be reviewed again from within; in this case, from the subterranean or intraterrestrial world, a dark hell that opens up from under that green inferno.

The many years that have gone by since the legend first came out and the lack of evidence through time have led many to regard the

The Namangoza River surrounded by thick jungle

matter as false. This is particularly true for Ecuadorians, who have not believed in this phenenomenon ever since it first came to light.

The Basque-Argentinian speleologist Julio Goyén Aguado, a good friend of mine, may be the reason I stuck with this enigma for so long—him and the Scottish engineer Stanley Hall, who always thought those studying the Tayos were ugly ducklings with the potential to become swans. (Later on I would understand the meaning behind that expression.) This book is not a biography of them, but I couldn't have written it without talking about the life and work of the protagonists of the last three decades of this saga.

EARLY MADNESS
FOR THE TAYOS MYSTERY

My interest in the Tayos can be seen in my first book *Mundos paralelos* (Parallel worlds), where a brief chapter mentions Julio Goyén Aguado, one of the individuals responsible for the diffusion of the story of the Tayos back in the late seventies. Aguado first contacted me through some mutual friends. I timidly arrived at his office and met a sober-looking man who seemed to be angry with me. To write that chapter, I had extracted his comments from 1969 for a magazine called *2001: Periodismo de Anticipación* (2001: the journalism of anticipation), in which he had talked about the lost continent of Lemuria and its connection to the Andes. He had said: "The spiritual masters who worked on the path of good started recording precious chronicles and documents of the library of Lemuria to preserve the scientific and spiritual knowledge of the history of Earth. They are the ones who possess the secrets that are the legacy of men in South America."

In our conversation, Aguado told me that many of the things mentioned in that article didn't really happen that way. As I came to learn more about the topic over time, and as my friendship with him grew, I would understand that fantastic realism could better describe reality than a distorted or surreal image of it.

Aguado was a wonderful human being in every sense, one of those magical people who are so hard to find, and his work remains tinted with enchanting genius. Our twenty years of friendship went by very fast, maybe because of my self-exile and my rare trips to my home country. Fortunately, in the last years of his life we reconnected, and the friendship we had started years before grew even more.

Even if others who came into the picture tried to downplay Aguado's leading role in the story of the Tayos Caves, his presence and the enigma around him remain unforgettable. Without his influence, it is possible that Ecuador and the Tayos would never have become a part of my destiny. There are countless letters, documents, and witnesses to corroborate this claim. The mysterious Juan Moricz would have never gone to Ecuador without Aguado, and if Moricz had never gone on this journey, the story, the legends, and the discovery of the caves would have been forgotten. Without Moricz there would be no book by von Däniken, and this story would be just another undisclosed tale of the Andean heights, valleys, and jungles, in wait of new explorers. Without von Däniken, there would have been no Stanley Hall, and the cave would not have gotten international attention. And without Hall, the story would not have been complicated by the involvement of Petronio Jaramillo Abarca, who originally claimed that he was taken into the cave by a childhood friend.

The story of the Tayos belongs to Latin America, not to Britain, in spite of the work of Stanley Hall. Unfortunately, what is written or visually documented in English has more international scope. Even Hispanics give greater value to texts written in a language other than Spanish.

In 1997 I spent a lot of time with Aguado, maybe because a part of me knew I would never see him again, but also because we had the same exploratory ideals. He was excited to go back to the caves and had promised he would try to get the necessary permits so that we could reach the chamber of the metallic library.

Back then I was trying, with superhuman patience, to convince the Latin division of the Discovery Channel to help us with a filmed expedition. I didn't know that trying to convince both the Latin and the American divisions of the importance of the subject was a difficult crusade that would make me feel I was casting pearls before swine, as so often happens when you try to make a program about culture these days. I later learned that the topics showcased in the Latin and American divisions were, and still are, controlled mostly by the channel's European division.

I was moved by Aguado's humility when I told him about my endeavor. He simply asked me if I could take him with me on my Ecuadorian expedition. Two years of presentations and negotiations went by, but when everything was almost ready, he died in an accident in the Argentinian Andes.

In 1970 Aguado founded the Argentinian Center for Speleology (its Spanish acronym is CAE). This was the same year my exploration of the Brujas Cave (also known as the Witches' Cave) in Malargüe, Mendoza, Argentina, took place. I had my speleological "initiation" around 1980, and I did my first small expedition, a preamble to what would come years later. During that trip, Aguado and the members of his team made the following statement to the local media: "Subterranean caverns connected with Ecuador will be studied in Mendoza."

Since my first meeting with Julio in the winter of 1979, the subject of the connection between the Brujas and the Tayos Caves was as common as hearing that under the mountain range these tunnels connected countries and continents, and that beings from a benign brotherhood lived among them and watched over the destiny of humankind.

The newspaper that covered the expedition also said that "the whole American continent, from the Rocky Mountains to Patagonia, could be connected by artificial caves. If confirmed, this would be the greatest discovery ever made, a discovery that would undoubtedly change the history of humanity. The expedition will include specialists in anthropology, archaeology, geology, philology, and speleology with the hopes of finding one of the sites of the subterranean network located in Ecuador."

MY FIRST TWO EXPEDITIONS

My journals are the best way to help the reader understand the story of the Tayos because they vividly illustrate what I experienced and explored. It took me almost three decades to get to Ecuador and the Tayos Caves. This odyssey has shown me that, like the rivers that cross the Amazon basin from north to south and west to east, the passing of days is unstoppable. (To see maps I have made showing the various areas explored, see plates 1 and 2.)

Notes from My Travel Journal

I was like a teenager coming back from his first Andean trip, in love with the "blue mountains," as I called them back then—words that remain with me even today. The first trip to the Andes changed me in many ways.

I grew up in Argentina closer to my European roots, but I was lucky enough to have a couple of mentors who awoke in me the need to look west, deep into the South American continent, a trapeze of ancestral lands that made me daydream of the dawn of time.

These dreams are still the same today. Even after the rivers and gales of time and space have swollen my face and given me wrinkles, I am still thirsty for wind and sun and the Andes. Those holy mountains that pour out their rivers, the blood of the earth and life, running to the interior of the maternal womb—that was where I wanted to go. I went there with a purpose: to find the truth and break the spell.

Those mountains helped me follow that dream to find the truth. To accomplish this, I didn't need to take hallucinogenic plants because I had broken my ego decades ago and more recently, maybe for thousands of years, trying to find the light at the end of the tunnel of truth. I had died a thousand deaths in quest of this truth and had always been resurrected.

These expeditions aimed to find the lost steps in the search of mystery and to corroborate if my friend Julio had lied to us about what he saw when he visited the Tayos Caves with Juan Moricz in 1968, or if he had had a peak experience.* Sometimes we need these uncertainties to be able to move forward and to reach a better future—one that stems from a cryptic past whose glories, more often than not, we don't know how to interpret.

The stars still shine above us and send us messages we don't understand. Every day we find things from the past. We leave them there, or we are moved to display them in museum cabinets, as dead as they were before their discovery.

I found this was common with the topic of the Tayos. Those who knew sometimes talked about it, sometimes kept quiet, but in the end they didn't know and were not completely sure if their experience had been real. I sailed against the rivers of uncertainty, the lack of resources, and contrived disinformation to finally get there decades after my initial impulse.

It was a sublime obsession, or maybe a recurring madness. The grail was and is in the depths, and I had to look at it at least once. That is what I did in the end, and that gave me the temporary satisfaction of fulfilling a disregarded duty.

My work has been lonely, and I haven't had many allies. I didn't need governments, or crowns, or official science to accomplish my task. People tried to make me give up (even those who had supported me and claimed to be my friends); they told me to put it off until the area was more at peace. But that area had always been hostile, and it would continue being so. I have to thank them for having recognized my decisiveness in reaching the goal.

I have never been surer that the mind and the heart shape our

---

*My recent meeting with the widow and the daughter of Julio Goyén Aguado offered some evidence that Julio was telling the truth about what he saw. His wife and daughter remembered Julio's original experience, his excitement and thrill after going into the cave and the moment he found the metallic library.

reality, and that our intention is the secret formula we all have for accomplishing our tasks—the fire we can't measure or contain, but which exists within us as a part of our human magic, of our lineage as terrestrial yet divine beings.

This essay has been written by a man in search of truth, a man who, like the Little Prince, believes that "what is essential is invisible to the eye." And if I keep on believing, maybe what my friend Julio Goyén Aguado and his friend Juan Moricz told us could still be true in spite of all the doubts and the rivers of time that have endlessly gone by over the same place. This is where my expeditions and observations begin. They corroborate some beliefs and destroy others.

The only thing I can say is that I am free, and that nature is above us with its spectacular caverns and forests. That life force is much more important than any legacy of gold, copper, or brass. We are of the same essence, and we all come from one human being who may have had extrahuman origins. Today we are still here, with a sun that warms us and prepares us to wait for the next day with the hope or desire to evolve a little, to ascend, to be better human beings. An awareness of an American past that was ahead of its time may give us the strength to project ourselves ahead, toward an uncertain but exciting future.

Finally, Ecuador (2006)

Just like the last time, this time it wasn't easy to get here because of the delays that had taken so long. This time too many factors coincided. I had the mission of finding more evidence to validate my research of the Masma* culture that I had studied since the early eighties, and I knew that in Ecuador, as in all the Andes, there were more keys to unravel.

---

*The name *Masma* was coined by researcher Daniel Ruzo to describe a megalithic ancient civilization skilled in cyclopean constructions and lost techniques continued by the Incan cultures.

Even if I had relocated to Europe and I had found my soul mate there, the restlessness aroused by an incomplete task would not leave me. It was more than just destiny or karma. There was something I had to begin so that I could end other things that were hanging by a thread between realities and dreams.

So after many letters back and forth with adventurer and treasure hunter Stan Grist, we both agreed it was time to do an expedition to the cave, thirty years after Stanley Hall's international expedition of 1976. At the same time, I was still preparing the documentary I had been working on since the mideighties with my longtime friends the Alvarados, from Ecuavisa, the Ecuadorian TV channel.

I arrived in Quito on a rainy day, at the time of the elections. A part of me was finding it difficult to recover from a personal loss I had recently suffered. It meant surrendering and dying before moving on; and that syndrome of the explorer who can't find his source of gold was showing its symptoms in advance.

With Grist we started reviewing the texts and clues from Stanley Hall's book *Tayos Gold,* and we compared it to our own notes. He was looking for answers and had met my friend Aguado. Destiny had taken me to Buenos Aires just one year before I saw Aguado for the last time. Our destinies met and brought us together, all of us who had been and still are a part of the web of the Tayos.

We were supposed to go to the coordinates Hall had published as the real ones for locating the golden library that had eluded Moricz and followers in previous expeditions over several decades.

Before our departure Grist and I got to meet and interview Petronio Jaramillo Abarca's widow. In the late sixties and early seventies, the writer and researcher Pino Turolla had interviewed Jaramillo, who was the self-proclaimed first person to discover the treasure of the Tayos Caves. Grist and I had come to the conclusion that Jaramillo was a key character, because we had both read Turolla's book and had compared notes through the years.

This is why we headed toward Guayaquil for some interviews and to maybe come closer to Coangos, the Shuar town closest to the main caves of the same names. There we learned of the ideas of Gastón Fernández Borrero, Hernán Burgos Stone, and Monica Williams, who were part of the story of the Tayos through Juan Moricz. Before the Coangos expedition, I realized the relationship with Grist would not survive such a long journey into the jungle, because we were both too used to traveling alone. I still tried to invite him to join the first expedition, but my associates from Ecuavisa could not find a place for him. This was better for all of us, because the expedition would not get to its destination, and we had limited space and other inconveniences typical of jungle explorations. (Later, Grist would erase our experiences together from public commentaries and turned into a renegade.)

So I got to Guayaquil, to the Hotel Rizzo where Moricz lived for two decades until his death in 1991.

The Bizarre Death of Juan Moricz

Moricz spent his last days at Hotel Rizzo in Guayaquil, where he had lived since 1968, when it was called the Continental. In 1991 he was found dead in the bathroom of room 409.

Moricz talked a lot with the hotel's bellboys and waiters. He told Joel Condo, one of the managers, that "there was a treasure in the cave that was millions of years old." Moricz was always late with the rent, so one time the manager pushed him to pay, and this angered Moricz. "Come over here, I want to show you what I have," Moricz said. He hailed a cab, and they went to the intersection of Aguirre and Malecón. The manager followed him to a fifth floor, where Moricz had his office, and there Moricz showed him some rocks in a glass cabinet with geological samples, maps, and photographs. "I have golden ingots in the Bank of Uruguay, and at the moment I am waiting to finish a contract with the Japanese."

Cesar Gavilanes, the head waiter at the Continental at the time, said, "Moricz was very quiet; he was more Argentinian than Hungarian. In his last years a woman much younger than him looked after him. When he passed away, she came while the superintendent and the commissioner drew up the death certificate."

One day when I was interviewing the hotel personnel, something weird happened in the room. The bathroom mirror of the room where Moricz had stayed up until his heart attack cracked for no reason at all, hurting the bellboy's hand. When I got to the room, I found blood everywhere, even on the cracked pieces of mirror on the floor. The people at the hotel believed this happened because I had bothered the *muertito* or "little dead guy," as the personnel described him. This coincided with my intuition that Juan had left us with many unresolved issues; maybe he was still roaming the Earth.

There were many speculations around his death. People talked about curses and urban legends; they had exalted him and vilified him, but his presence remained. Not too far away, the iguanas at the plaza slept under the sun, just like the day Moricz had died, taking a thousand secrets with him to the grave.

The tomb of Juan Moricz

Andreas Faber-Kaiser* said that it would be good to search the grave, because it was hard for him to believe the Hungarian was no longer with us, and he also believed that Moricz's work would be left unfinished. Faber-Kaiser was suspicious as to whether Moricz was buried beneath his tomb marker and thought the tomb should be opened to verify Moricz's death. In Guayaquil, I found some of Moricz's friends, who gave me more information. The most important ones were the Peña Matheus brothers, the true patrons of the life and adventures of the explorer of the Tayos Caves.

Back in Quito I would continue to finding more links of the chain of events that allowed me to rebuild Moricz's life from the moment he arrived at the Ecuadorian capital and other places in the country between 1964 and 1991. So the dots started connecting after every meeting I had with the other protagonists of the story.

I met a member of the Rosicrucian order, who said Moricz had shown them some plates that did not belong to those of Father Crespi. Professor Soto remembers seeing Moricz showing his colleagues a stack of golden plates piled one over the other; he had wrapped them in Kraft paper under his arm.

Another pillar of support would be Jorge Salvador Lara, whom I met researching the Jesuit Library. He was one of the first persons Moricz visited when he first arrived in Ecuador, and he admitted that the Hungarian's search could have some truth behind it, even if it broke with the dogmas of traditional history.

The First Expedition:
Notes from the Travel Journal

During my first three months in Ecuador I researched the Tayos system in the eastern part of the country. For this I did two joint

---

*Andreas Faber-Kaiser (1944–1994) was a research journalist and author of *Fantastic Realism*. He interviewed Moricz in the eighties and tried to get to the caves by himself. His experience was told in a classic article called "La cruz del Diablo" (The Devil's cross), published by the magazine *Más Allá de la Ciencia* (Beyond science).

expeditions, the first one with the support of GITFA (Tactical Intervention Group of the Air Force of Ecuador), which focused on the caverns of the Morona-Santiago province (plate 3 shows a photo of this area).

These members of the Ecuadorian Air Force were trained for all types of terrain, but the members who went with me had not been specifically trained in climbing, nor did they have experience in caves.

The main Tayos Cave was the setting of Moricz's 1969 expedition for CETURIS (the Ecuadorian Corporation of Tourism) as well as the setting for the international (or British-Ecuadorian) expedition of 1976. When we tried to get there from the Coangos River, I discovered that the situation with the natives was very unstable. There was also a military director in our group who was too cautious (he was a desk officer; as has happened for centuries in the armed forces, unpopular officers end up being sent to the jungle), and he wanted to avoid risks more than he wanted to reach the objective.

When we returned to Macas, I was informed there had been an attack in Sucua. There we interviewed Colonel Marco Ortiz and Governor Joaquín Estrella. In the end, my expedition helped create a connection for Ecuavisa, because this network, like all those from the main cities, did not cover the eastern part of Ecuador. We were informed that the police had been attacked when they tried to evict a Shuar group that was invading lands and properties. The place had been the Bumbaza/Wamba Center, 20.4 miles in the direction of Gualaquiza.

Since we could not cross the Namangoza River, we went back to Macas. After a night of frustration and insomnia, I decided we would explore the other Tayos Cave. Little did I know this cave was the one for which Stanley Hall, a previous explorer of the cave, had given the coordinates for in his new online notes and in a book he had recently self-published.

The purpose of my first expedition was to verify Stanley Hall's declarations, as Hall was a controversial follower of Juan Moricz's theories. But at the beginning of 2005, Hall surprised those interested in the metallic library by believing Jaramillo's account of the caves and moving the location of the treasure from one cavern to another located 62 miles away.

After twenty-seven years of research, I finally decided to begin the first part of my explorations with the most novel aspect of the topic: the declarations that the library was in one of the caverns of the Pastaza River, and not in the Coangos, as everyone had believed since the late seventies, and where the expeditions of 1969 and 1976 had focused, the latter of which was organized by Hall himself. All those expeditions concluded without ever finding the metallic library that had been seen by Moricz and Aguado in 1968.

Second Expedition (The Pastaza River): Notes from the Travel Journal

The expedition managed to go almost all the way to the bottom of the Chumbitayo Cave located close to the Pastaza River (see plate 4).

We photographed and studied the behavior of the tayos, birds considered sacred by the indigenous Shuar people since ancient times. The Shuar still hunt the squabs in nests found in the high cavern walls.

Along the subterranean river, I found several unexplained sculptures that appeared to be from the Masma culture, which reminded me of my repeated explorations for similar structures on Peru's Marcahuasi Plateau. These sculptures are shaped like condors or pigeons, piranha-like fish, which are abundant in the area, and a combined bird-fish that is common in Shuar iconography. During our expeditions to the Chumbitayo Cave (which, Hall believed, had been where Jaramillo initially found the library and the metallic treasure), other sculptures that stand out are birds and other creatures, such as mammals or canines, chasing after them. Among these anomalies we could also observe other animals, such as a dolphin (which could very well be a river dolphin), and a spectacular piranha sculpted on a low embankment. Its perfection and its location, leveled over the subterranean river, make it impossible to say that it is a natural occurrence caused by erosion. This too reminded me of the Masma sculptures in the Marcahuasi Plateau, where figures of marine creatures, such as seals, sea lions, or fish, are undoubtedly found in an area of small lakes that only fill up on certain periods of the year.

Another geological anomaly was an anvil-like stone that protruded from one of the walls of the subterranean river. This was unusual and could not be explained by natural causes (see plate 5 to see me inspecting the rock of this cave). These elements are also found in the Tayos Cave at Coangos, such as the angular stone and the brick and polished arches, elements that remain unexplained, even though the British-Ecuadorian expedition of 1976 attempted to describe them as formations caused by fluvial erosion. (You can read their report on page 152.)

In one part of the caves, thanks to the observant eye of my photography director, Mathias Spatz, we discovered an area with golden metallic reflections with perfectly delineated rectangles that stood out and may have contributed to the legend of the gold plates in the Tayos Caves (see plate 6).

Could these golden swaths be what was glimpsed by those explorers of the past? Logic and the intrinsic truth don't always apply in the universe of the Tayos. Perhaps the explorers before me reasoned the treasure of the caves into existence; but then again perhaps they did not. What I saw and what they saw may be completely unrelated, or our observations may indeed be linked. Perhaps we will never know for certain, unless undeniable evidence is unearthed, but we can continue to wonder, debate, and dream. The pages that follow may introduce you to the story of the Tayos for the first time. If you are a seasoned researcher, may they illuminate your quest.

2

The Ecuadorian Jungle

The Cradle of Civilization

Going deep into the Amazon jungle in Ecuador is as daring a task today as it was one or two hundred years ago. Even if today's traditions are not as wild as they were back then, time seems to have stood still. After years expended in that jungle's terrain, space and time are not the same, not for me and not for the people around me related to the story and its different narratives. Over time, places change spatially, and the way we remember them changes too.

In 1539 Gonzalo Pizarro, brother of Francisco Pizarro, conqueror of the Inca Empire, led an expedition toward a kingdom sought by Captain Francisco de Orellana, who had gone back to civilization, defeated after fighting against a tribe of women—the famous Amazons who were tall, blonde, blue-eyed, and not very friendly toward the opposite sex.

Pizarro and Orellana were searching for the lost golden city of Paititi, deep in the jungle, a search that would continue for five hundred years and still goes on today. According to the British historian John Dyson, Christopher Columbus was not looking for a route to the Indies, but for a land of gold that would coincide with the maps of Piri Reis, the nephew

22

of Admiral Kemal Reis, who served under Suleiman the Magnificent.*

THE SACRED GEOMETRY
OF ECUADOR

The Ecuadorian Andes are the cradle of the mystery that begins at the equator, which guides us toward sacred sites, pyramids, tumuli— and the Tayos Caves.

There are stories from sacred history, excerpts of an intricate astrological record of the Cycles of the Ages. The policy of the Christian church was to destroy the documents of the ancient system of spiritual science in order to suppress the practice of archaeoastronomy and proper astronomy, which is derived from astrology and which studied the effects of the stars on geography and human nature.

The Chinese called these lines the *lung-mei,* and they extended all over the world. In Australia and North America the "dragon lines" are also creation paths, enchanted by the gods, by the primitive snake, and by the ancestral guardian of all living things. In some parts of the world these dragon lines can be seen from the air. Although their origin is very ancient, not many people who live around them recognize them.

For example, the famous Nazca lines and similar lines that extend throughout the north of Chile and Bolivia are sun-oriented paths set up in such a way that travelers walking in certain lines during the equinox or solstice could see the sun rising or hiding over the right line of the horizon.

---

*The 1513 map of Piri Reis, admiral of the Ottoman Empire, continues to be a great cartographic mystery. It was traced using an unknown advanced technology and was also accessed by Christopher Columbus before and during the discovery of the Americas.

THE MYSTERY OF THE SHUAR (JÍBAROS)

Being in Amazonian Ecuador was not a matter of mere tourism for me; it was essential. A cycle that should have ended twenty-five years before opened up before me in a green abyss, in front of an impenetrable and deadly setting. To understand the geography I was going into, I first and foremost had to understand the Shuar, a tribe who are often called the Jíbaro (a name they object to, because it is a disrespectful corruption of the indigenous noun Shuar and represents them as primitive).

Who are the Shuar? How did they come to be? It is almost impossible to answer this question of how they originated. There is an undoubted linguistic similarity of the Jíbaro language in its Shuar, Achuar, Awajún, and Wampi forms to European languages such as Hungarian (Magyar), one of the oldest languages in Central Europe. This similarity was discovered by Juan Moricz in the seventies, and it certainly is a contribution to ethnographic linguistics that cannot be denied academically, since it is studied in universities around the globe.

It is clear the Shuar have undeniable similarities with other races from the Amazon and Asia. But the Shuar did not leave behind their history in writing, and their archaeological remains are few, unless the missing metallic libraries end up being identified as creations of the ancestors of the Jíbaro race.

Official anthropologists such as Jijón y Caamaño, influenced by the European school, connected migrations to the Paleolithic, Mesolithic, and Neolithic periods. There are three clear waves during the Neolithic period:

1. The marginal and independent tribes, which were heavily oppressed and almost destroyed by a second tribe.
2. The Arawaks, whose center of propagation was the mouth of the Amazon River, spreading to the island of Marajó,

Brazilian Guyana, Argentina, Bolivia, and Peru. They had a very wide dispersion radius, from Florida to Panama.

3. The Caribs. Their propagation center began at the Orinoco basin. After spreading throughout South America, they defeated the Arawaks, who were left scattered in groups that disappeared after their dispersion.

It is possible one of these Arawak tribes merged with one of the first migration streams. This could have been the group with the Chibchan language, or the Yunga, Puruhá, or Puruhá-Mochica, which was spoken by the Puruhá groups that lived on the hillsides of the Chimborazo, and the Mochica group from the Peruvian region of Pativilca, with a language that was not extinct until the beginning of the twentieth century.

Later on, the belligerent Caribs tore apart the Arawak colonies, and the survivors traveled to eastern Ecuador, where they merged with one of the established towns of the Puruhá-Mochica. The Jíbaros were born from this convergence.

According to Jorge Salvador Lara, the Jíbaros came from the east, and they settled next to the Marañón River, but they also wandered into the highlands and the Loja province, where they settled as the Paltas. According to this theory, the Shuar language would be the result of the merger of an original Arawak language with one of the Puruhá-Mochica. When the Incas entered the picture, the Jíbaro groups of the Pastaza region might have been transformed into Quechuas, as was the case with the Canelos or the Alamas. The ancient Arawaks traveled along the Amazon to the east, but they left traces of their settlements throughout this ancestral route.

One theory states that once *Homo sapiens* stood out from the other species by our ability to use our hands and separate the thumb from the rest of the fingers to use handle tools, we dared to venture into the unknown. It is possible that in those times the distances between Asia and the Bering Strait were not as inhospitable for intercontinental travel as they are now, and that, after five thousand years as nomads, the travelers decided to venture to new horizons. It is possible that among them a group of hunters and gatherers crossed. Some scholars link them to the Koreans, but we can also call them the Proto-Shuar.

Proto-Asian migrations started to move toward America in migration waves with pauses of ten thousand years. The forefathers of the Arawaks used rafts and primitive boats to populate the Antilles, to later move toward what today is the plateau of Colombia, to Venezuela; still in rafts, they reached Marajó Island, at the mouth of the Amazon River, where they would spread through most of the South American continent. Others decided to take the rafts and canoes south, bordering the Pacific coast. (Books by Emilio Estrada and Paulina Lederberger can give you more information about this.) This is how, more than eight thousand years ago, the Shuar proto-race landed on the Manabí beaches and continued south, influencing many of the coastal names.

During the screening of a documentary on the life of the Achuar, the wife of the Japanese karate fighter Kasuya Mayahira, a linguistic expert in the languages of her region (Okinawa), was surprised to discover she understood about 50 percent of the expressions, which were similar to those that had been spoken on her island since ancient days. Even the architecture of the houses was the same. Others from Moricz's generation who supported the idea of the transoceanic migration of cultures include Thor Heyerdahl, Vito Alzar, and Betty Meggers.

THE POPULATION OF THE ECUADORIAN MESOPOTAMIA

Around the year 4000 BCE the Proto-Shuar settled in the basin of the Marañón River of the high Amazon. There, prehistoric pilgrims did not take long to move from Loja to Zamora, following the Marañón to get to what today is the Cóndor mountain range, and the great rivers: the Morona, the Santiago, and the Cenepa. Around the year 2500 BCE, in the valley of Hoang Ho or Coang Ho (note the phonetic similarities with the word "Coangos"), the Chinese civilization was being born. At the same time the Jíbaros started to go upriver to find food.

These were the times of goddess Nunkui, when the Shuar became horticulturist travelers. The use of fire, hunting, and fruit and vegetable collection were perfected. By controlling fire, the first canoes were cut and carved. The ancestral Shuar ate *unkuch-eep* leaves, a sort of wild lettuce, and *wawa*, a tree bark that they also used for tightening rafts.

The Shuar population multiplied, and it grew past its ability to sustain itself. This led to divisions between family groups, which slowly became tribes. These formed the four groups of the Jíbaro nation.

SHUAR MYTHOLOGY AND TRADITIONS

Nunkui was the first Shuar in the world. At first she was a human, like all of us, but then she became a goddess and chose the Tayos Cave as her home. To this cave she brought women, children, and even dogs. Sunki appeared afterward; he was divine too.

Today, the dwellers in the caves do not visit the lower paths. The Shuar and white people today live on the upper paths, where we can still observe the steps of men, women, and children, Nunkui's followers. She inhabited the upper gallery amid luxury, gold, and precious stones. We cannot go into her lair, because we would be punished right away.

In 1976 Moricz wrote in his diary, "The Shuar inhabit the area where the Tayos Caves are located. Their religious traditions confirm that these caves are the dwelling of their god, a supreme being praised by the first inhabitants in eastern Ecuador and their descendants. Their god is eternal, but it is unknown if they believe he has a human shape with a body, or if he is simply a spirit, a soul, to whom his children, between April and June, go down to pay tribute through ceremonies of unknown nature, and also to hunt for *tayo* meat, which is rich in proteins."

The Shuar also established within their culture the common concept of the central pole and established rites similar to the Sun Dance of the native North Americans, such as the Lakotas, Dakotas, Sioux, and Blackfeet. According to their stories, Nunkui would go up the central pole, and from there, the strength of the *uwi* fruit would fill the pots. This legend takes shape in the traditional descent and ascent from the Tayos Caves when the oilbirds are harvested.

The Shuar are also known as the "people of the sacred waterfalls" because of the many waterfalls in their region. The powerful spirits or souls, the Arutam, reside in those waterfalls and waters, providing energy and the warrior spirit. Their dwelling is an initiation site for the young; there they try to understand the destiny of men.

To reach the waterfalls, you need to be respectful. The *uwishin* (shamans) fast five days before, and walk slowly, drinking *natem* (ayahuasca or *Banisteriopsis caapi*) and simulating the sounds of birds. When they reach the waterfalls, they hit a stone behind the fall, waiting for a signal from the water. When this opens to invite them in, the Arutam initiate contact, and the rituals take place. They fast as they leave the place, and they must not look back, because if they see blood instead of water, it is certain that bad omens, or even death, will come.

The Achuar, like the Shuar, have superstitions about killing animals. Hunting when there was no need would presage the death of a child in less than a year. Killing a capybara would lead one or several women related to the killer to commit adultery.

The myths and legends depict the inner world of these tribal groups, which always moved between destruction and restoration. This is why their stories about death are also about birth. When you visit their lands, you see the futility of life: one moment you think you are in the dream of a butterfly illuminated by the rays of light, the next you are being wounded by the foliage.

Waterfalls of all shapes and sizes create sanctuaries surrounded by forest, and you reach them by following hidden paths with moss-covered stones and steep slopes. The link with the liquid element goes deep. In fact, when a Shuar dies, he dissipates into water drops until he reaches the clouds.

One of their best-kept myths explains the Shuar cosmovision fully: The world we live in is not real; it is just a step before getting to the real one, and ayahuasca or datura are the hallucinogenic plants used to reach it. These are the doors used to reach reality from our daily unreality. Using them in an appropriate dosage also helps one to be reconciled with oneself after emotional turmoil or existential distress.

The real world is also recognized as the hidden or the supernatural world, and only the uwishin or shaman knows it well, because he has seen it many times. He is a wise man who can interpret what he sees in the great beyond, thus discovering the origins of disease and how to cure it. He is a man of great strength in the community, who has achieved this power with the accumulation of the power of the Arutam.

The way to reach the Arutam is transmitted from generation to generation. Every Shuar child follows the instructions of an older and wiser man, the *UTN* Shuar. They venture together into the jungle for one, two, or three days. The older man tells him his life experiences, and how he lives. He shows him the teachings of the jungle, he talks to him about the plants and animals, and he shows him they have a life and soul. They hunt and fish, so the child learns the rules and the teachings of life from a master. When he turns eleven, the child must fast and enter the jungle with an uwishin, a shaman, until he finds the sacred waterfall.

When they get there, they build the uwishin hut and then prepare to drink ayahuasca. The wise man reviews everything that happened on their journey through the jungle, and he talks to the child about what he will experience in his dreams. He will see things from the past, the present, and the future. When they drink ayahuasca, the young man will tell his dreams to the uwishin, who will help interpret them and find the Arutam.

For the Shuar, an uwishin is the shaman or the person of knowledge and power. The uwishin are men who can cause fear in people because they can use the magical arts and their knowledge of ancestral plants and brews to do good or evil, to heal or kill.

The term uwishin comes from *uwin*, which is a palm tree commonly used as a symbol of the Amazon cultures. It was widely used for its fruit, which could serve as food or to produce chicha, a fermented beverage. Its wood could be used to build houses and to make different weapons, such as bows, arrows, and blowpipes.

A linguistic relationship could be established between the meaning of the palm arrows sent by the uwishin to their enemies to harm or even kill them and the shamanic practices of the Quechuas, who call the Shuar shamans *chonteros* (palmers). There is an extensive magical ritual exchange between these two groups. This is why many Shuar specialize under Quechua shamans or vice versa. The evil or disease is produced when these magical arrows are sent by the uwishins through the help of spirits, or through insects with stingers, by which they transmit their evil arrows.

Shamans are often hired to commit one of these attacks or to repel one. It is known that the power of the shamans was used in the wars between Shuar groups. The Amazon indigenous people claim that when these arrows hit someone, that person would be harmed, then weakened, and then would fall sick, and if not properly healed (meaning that the arrow was not removed) would die. The only one who can remove these arrows and heal the person is another uwishin.

To avoid being hurt, the Shuar take ayahuasca and datura, which are magical plants with great power, prepared in rituals to prevent disease, offer protection from attacks, and enable movement from a mundane plane to a magical healing plane.

Ayahuasca is at the heart of the shamanic ritual. The healing processes around the ingestion of this hallucinogen are directly related to the state of the uwishin, who fasts for long periods of time to locate and remove the arrows sent by enemies. The fasting lasts about ten hours; during this time they are only allowed to eat small amounts of yucca, plantain, and chicha, aside from liquid tobacco and certain amounts of alcohol.

In general, the ceremonies take place at night, because this is the ideal space for connecting to the magical world. According to Shuar beliefs, this is when the spirits and magical animals walk on our lands, so the brew should be consumed between 7 and 8 p.m., although the preparation is done earlier, because several hours of boiling are needed to activate the alkaloids in the plants.

LEGENDS SPECIFIC TO THE TAYOS CAVES

The Tayos Gorgon

The wizard Rosendo Ujukma tells the legend of the Coangos region. A Shuar woman betrayed her husband, and when he caught her red-handed, he wanted to pierce her with his spear. The woman escaped from the fury of her husband. She fled far away and wandered aimlessly through the forest until she reached a stream. She followed the water until it reached the opening of a cave. She was hungry because she hadn't eaten at all, so she caught a tayo bird and ate it, finding its meat delicious. When she found many of these birds, she ran back to her husband with a bird in hand to give him the good news and hoping to be forgiven. The husband, excited to hear the good news his wife just brought him, told the other members of the tribe. They all went to the cave and ate to their heart's content; afterward they celebrated the discovery by getting drunk.

Inside the cave, a young man took a sparrow hawk's egg and ate it. The others followed, eating eggs from other species, and they were all transformed into the species of the eggs they devoured. This is why all the animals now found in the Jíbaro lands come from the cave.

The first person to enter the Tayos Cave was a woman. The Shuar go down to the cave twice a year, after an arduous climb through vines and palm trees. The men must remain silent, while the women go down singing a song that can be translated as:

> *Oilbird, we come visit you;*
> *oilbird we come to catch you;*
> *oilbird you belong to us,*
> *because your death*
> *gives us life.*

Another story says that once, when Shuar men, women, and children went down to the cave to hunt birds, a pregnant woman was among them. She was so far along that when she wanted to get out, she couldn't. She stayed inside the cave and turned into stone. She is the rock we find at the end of the entrance corridor or chimney.

The Tiger and the Two Brothers

Two brothers got lost in the depths of the cave because their friends cut down the vine ladder. In their efforts to find the way out, they traveled their way into the upper cave, meaning the upper corridor. Their attempts to escape were useless, and they were resigned to their bad luck. Some tayos took pity on them and helped them climb through the mouth of the cave. They were barely out when a tiger suddenly appeared and ate one of the brothers. The survivor followed the tiger to an exit, and thanks to it, he saved himself.

This story is told on both the Ecuadorian and Peruvian sides of the border. Ethnographically, the Shuar have no borders. Furthermore, the border between Ecuador and Peru has long been disputed, going back to Spanish colonial times. Most recently, the dispute led to a military confrontation in 1995. The two countries summoned international arbitrators from Argentina, Chile, Brazil, and the United States. The verdict stated the border should remain in the summits of the Cóndor mountain range, and that the whole Cenepa River, and the 7,722 square miles of the Tiwinza region, belonged to Peru. It also granted 386 square miles to Ecuador for commemorative acts. Two ecological parks were created, with a larger area guaranteed for the Peruvian side.

There is no doubt that the geopolitical situation is connected to the destiny of the lost treasure of the Tayos. Through all these years of research and exploring, I came to the conclusion that no one knows exactly where the borders are between the two countries, both in relation to the caves and since the last war with Peru.

3

Golden Mysteries of the Andes

We Spaniards know a sickness that only gold can cure.

Hernando Cortés

S adly, most of the discoveries in the Americas were driven by the lust for gold. Even if many documents justify the Spanish conquest of the land in order to evangelize the natives, these same documents tell us that the real motivation behind their show of force was the hope for rapid riches. So in reality the conquistadors ventured into the Americas in a kind of gold rush.

The ceremony of the Guatavita *cacique* (chief) at a lake in the heights of Colombia gave origin to the legend of the El Dorado or the Golden Man, and the search for it began when there was no gold left. The explorer and cosmographer López de Velasco writes: "From the provinces that spoke of El Dorado we don't really know more than what has already been said, only that the discoveries were made around the Marañón River [the source of the Amazon], that the natives from those provinces went to Quito and Peru, and that some also reached the provinces of Río de la Plata. Many treasures have been found, which is common with every new discovery, and even if this one might be true, there is not enough evidence."

Even with the gold rush for the land of El Dorado, we found no evidence that the expeditions were searching for the actual Guatavita cacique; instead they seemed to be searching for mysterious regions erroneously called "El Dorado" or something synonymous. The explorers of the past were very much like the explorers of today in that all were searching for gold. The search for the treasure of the Tayos by Moricz's generation is akin to the contemporary search for other treasures related to El Dorado or Paititi.

For the transnational mining companies, the Amazon basins, especially the regions discussed in this book, are still a target for exploitation at the expense of the local ecology. The area of the Tayos Caves is close to what once was the Marañón region, which includes rivers that witnessed the most important expeditions of the gold rush.

Diego de Ordas's search for El Dorado is not mentioned in documents related to that expedition, but it is included in Martín Fernández de Enciso's work *Summa de Geografía* (1539): "Diego de Ordas arrived to the Marañón River with the intent to begin his discoveries there because a couple of days before he met four natives in a canoe who found two emeralds, one as large as a fist; and they said that a few day's walk up river was a rock consisting of that stone."

Ordas also heard about a place and a tribe called the Meta, which was supposed to be very rich. When explorers reached this region, they found riches that belonged to the northern territories of what would become the Spanish province called the New Kingdom of Granada (present-day Colombia, Venezuela, Ecuador, and Panama) where emeralds, gold, cotton, and salt were abundant. Higher up the Marañón, Ordas's expedition caught a native and showed him the golden ring of the governor. After being tortured, the native told them there was more of that brilliant material behind the mountain range that opened up to the left of the river.

On the Ecuadorian coast we find certain similar elements. Coaque Bay, where Pizarro's ships docked in 1524, was originally called Ccori-Haqque, which means "man of gold." (The people who worked and valued gold settled along the coast more than in the jungle.) In the Tayos Cave at Coangos, many golden artifacts were found, as well as *Spondylus* (spiny oysters), which came from the coast. In the Parima region (in today's Brazil), the Spaniards saw domes of solid gold, silver obelisks, and many other things that years later Alexander von Humboldt, one of the first to describe the subterranean world of South America from Venezuela to Ecuador, would say were mistaken interpretations of mica rocks.

After Humboldt's travels in the Americas (from 1799 to 1804), Percy Fawcett (1867–1925) was one of the next explorers to venture into this part of the world. I have been fascinated by Fawcett's Brazilian explorations ever since I read the picturesque book edited and illustrated by his son and called *Exploration Fawcett*, which was also published as *Lost Trails, Lost Cities*. Fawcett disappeared in 1925, as many unfortunate souls disappear when they wander in territories with hostile natives. Today many travelers and explorers keep disappearing for those same causes, in addition to the large number who come across illegal farmers who rule the edge of the jungle in the Andes and Amazon. Having traveled through the same countries Fawcett explored for most of his life—Brazil and Bolivia—I have found that the urge to solve the mystery of his disappearance has stayed with me to this day.

Fawcett derived his image as the great explorer of the twentieth century from a nineteenth-century romantic ideal, fostered by the British press, as they attempted to publicize great representative icons of their territorial expansionism. As a favorite of the Royal

Geographical Society (RGS), Fawcett was selected by the Bolivian government to create a topographic survey of the nation's borders.

When Fawcett came to South America, he already sensed that his final search was going to be for Atlantis and its lost colonies. A friend, the writer H. Rider Haggard—author of the classic *King Solomon's Mines*—had given him a statuette from the Andes, which represented a character that seemed biblical, like a pharaoh; some scholars even identified it as Noah.

At the age of fifty-three, after returning from World War I, Fawcett decided to dedicate his life to finding a citadel with subterranean channels and secret passageways whose existence some natives had confirmed in previous trips of his. He called it the Lost City of Z. Based on this data, he concluded the city could be located close to the Xingu and Araguaia Rivers up in the Roncador Range. So in 1924 Fawcett left from Cuaibá, in the Mato Grosso province, with his son and another young Englishman. The last news we have of him is a letter he sent to his wife on May 29. The mystery of his disappearance was left unsolved. His end started when he headed northeast instead of west, where he had been told there were gigantic cities like those of the Lost City of Z. He took no heed of the advice given by the last persons who saw him alive.

I believe Percy Fawcett walked past the borders of some Xingu tribes, who are known for their aggressiveness. He had run out of gifts with which to negotiate. After weeks being short of supplies in the midst of the wild, his expedition team, which included his teenage son, Jack, and a friend of his called Raleigh Rimell, failed to return to the civilized world.

In 1930 the American explorer George Miller Dyott was sent by a news agency to find Fawcett, dead or alive. He never found solid evidence of Fawcett's whereabouts or what really happened to him and his companions on their last expedition through the Mato Grosso. Yet there is no doubt that his expedition, and his disappearance, influenced the historical studies of the South American continent.

Perhaps Fawcett decided to stay in his final abode, where he transcended to a sort of mortal continuity, and survives in a parallel and subterranean world. Some believe Fawcett is alive in a subterranean kingdom, and that this place, known as Z, is part of an intricate tunnel system that begins under the Amazon jungle and connects to other equally mysterious settlements in the premountain and mountain ranges of the Andes. Brazilian authors believe Fawcett dwells inside the Roncador Range, where he enjoys the company of other important individuals from the past who also disappeared throughout the centuries.

My hypothesis is that the sources the English explorer heard and saw were a reflection of the legend of El Dorado or Paititi, but this time in a subterranean setting. As echoes of ancient true legends, the rumor of the Golden Lost Civilization was all along related to the Conquest of the Americas, and it lured in more modern explorers such as Fawcett and Moricz himself.

Maybe what Fawcett was searching for was discovered half a century later by Gene Savoy (1927–2007). This American explorer, journalist, and mystic from Washington State started exploring the Peruvian Andes in the 1950s, focusing on the central area of the Andes, and later ventured into the area now called Chachapoyas. In this region Savoy found cities that had been covered by undergrowth, like the Gran Pajaten, the Gran Vilaya, and Kuelap. These ruins were a part of a culture different from that of the Incas and pre-Incas. The Chachapoyas culture came from the east; it seems that they had crossed the Orinoco River and settled in the area. They had light skin, and some of their mummies even had reddish hair. Their tombs were elevated, they used clay sarcophagi, and they left behind a series of ideographic writings. Many of those symbols described the large vessels they used to cross unknown oceans, and what we believe was the Atlantic Ocean. This culture also built gigantic walls and structures throughout the mountains before the arrival of the Spaniards, whom they fought in bloody wars. The mystery behind them could explain why Fawcett felt drawn to explore the South American jungles. Fawcett had been searching for Atlantis and other lost cultures when he came upon this advanced civilization, and he intuited that they must have spread throughout America.

But what makes Fawcett stand out, and what connects him to us and to other explorers of the invisible, is that he had studied theosophy. Indeed his brother, Edward Douglas Fawcett, had helped the founder of this movement, H. P. Blavatsky, to write her masterpiece, *The Secret Doctrine.*

Juan Moricz had the same kind of intuition that Fawcett had. Like Fawcett, Moricz studied nineteenth-century metaphysics and occultism, which made him question the usual views of human origins. This pattern undoubtedly also affected Gene Savoy's explorations. None of these three explorers has so far been taken seriously by ethnography or anthropological sciences. Fawcett could never prove he was in a region that had been colonized by the descendants of Atlantis, just as Moricz could never prove the geological and linguistic anomalies in the Morona-Santiago region came from a cross between South American natives and the Magyars (Hungarians), as he believed. The same thing happened with Savoy, who believed the Chachapoyas could have been descended from the fleet of the Queen of Sheba, from the mythical kingdom of Ophir.

Gold was the element that linked these explorations. For centuries this factor has been one of the most primal forces that has fueled the interest behind the explorations. Moricz's epic saga, be it true or false, was driven by it.

At first, Savoy was searching for powers of rejuvenation, or for the power to stop time and space, which, he believed, originated in the temples, in the pyramid structures, or in the high peaks or hills that were synchronized with the power of the sun. Solar energy paired with stone and gold—a phenomenon that may have been the myth turned into reality by the pre-Incas and the Incas.

The sudden death of Savoy's son Jamil (1959–62) at a young age drowned him in desperation, which led him to get involved in a study that linked the Essenes with the New World; a civilization that also came from the Middle East, and which connected to King Solomon's mines and the kingdom of Ophir.

Phoenicians and Greeks built advanced vessels that were able to sail to the American coasts. They also had tools that today are considered state of the art, even if the antiquity of artifacts such as the Antikythera mechanism, found in the Aegean Sea, has not been proven yet.

The Phoenicians could be descendants of one of the cultures that sailed from America to the Middle East. Civilizations such as the Pelasgians, the Etruscans, and the Egyptians could be descendants of a very ancient tribe from the Andes and the Amazon. On Puná Island we found ancient settlements we could link to deities from the Middle East, such as Atum Baal.

There were several commercial routes from the Middle East to the Americas. Even if Columbus learned about these routes, few people knew they reached the Cape Verde Islands and the coast of Brazil.

The Manoa kingdom was located in the middle of what today is Brazil, where precious metals were as important as healing and hallucinogenic plants.

What today is the Gulf of Aqaba, where the Red Sea is located, used to be another route that sailed toward the Indian Ocean to cross the Pacific, and it arrived at what today are the Peruvian-Ecuadorian coasts, or equatorial America.

These commercial routes led to genetic crossings, and the techniques from the East were transported along with art and science. People settled, and the West mixed with the East.

However, it was the gold routes that moved the ancient world, and other worlds that were even more ancient.

The Bible mentions the gold of Ophir and Parvaim or Purvaim. Some read it as *Paruaim*, and it refers to the Peruvian coast that goes from Piura to the north of Chile: Arica.

Other scholars, such as Hector Burgos Stone, believe Ophir coincided with what was called the Golden Province in the Manta region, which today is Ecuador. Here even today we find the ancient mines that existed before the Incan and pre-Incan exploitations.

TREASURE IN THE MOUNTAINS

But the search for gold does not end with El Dorado and the land explored by Fawcett and Savoy. The Tayos are not the only places in this region said to hold vast amounts of treasure. The stories of the treasure of Atahualpa and the hunt for the Llanganates treasure also reflect glimmers of golden treasure. Andrés Fernández Salvador Zaldumbide believes the treasure is in a cave that has a dry stream. He believes everything is there, just as the treasure hunter Bartholomew Blane believed before him. Blane used to say that not even one thousand men could move the treasure from its location. These are not only solid gold pieces, it is said; some pieces have inlaid emeralds. The treasure came from Peru, where there are no emeralds, but these gems can be found in the eastern part of Ecuador, on the coast, and on the northwest side of the Napo River. Andrés Fernández Salvador Zaldumbide recalls:

In the 1950s I was about 12.5 to 18.5 miles from the Llanganates Parks, which had the perimeter of three or four soccer fields. This part of the mountain range is rich in marcasite, a mineral rich in iron oxide. The fascinating thing is that in Llanganates life continues in the dark, because plants grow with little light. History connects Huayna Capac with the Kingdom of Quito and the area called Pacaritambo, which is undoubtedly connected to or has the linguistic root of Paucartampu or Paucartambo. The cave is not far away, between Limón and Méndez. Let's throw a guess and say about 31 miles from the Coangos cave.

I remember Moricz wanted me to go with him and visit the Crespi museum. I wasn't surprised when he showed us a piece he considered to be really valuable, and it turned out to be a golden advertising figurine of the Michelin Man. In my opinion, the treasure of the Tayos is not related at all to the treasure in Llanganates.

Andrés Fernández Salvador Zaldumbide admits there is a synchronicity in the search for Atahualpa's treasure that interweaves with the Tayos Cave; especially the search and discovery of Moricz and his meeting with Jaramillo that same week. Andrés heard about the story when he was visiting an old German friend, Alfredo Moebius, who told him Jaramillo's story.

Andrés said Moricz was a con man who didn't discover Cumbaratza, an ancient mine Moricz exploited in the 1980s, because he kept silent for years at a time, and Moricz ended up self-destructing. Moricz and his lawyer lost the mine and unleashed a controversy still running to this day. Andrés also told me that the same week he met Moricz, Jaramillo called him on the phone to ask for his help to return to the cave he had been shown as a child. Jaramillo had a real fear of returning and to go into the place he said he needed grenades, machine guns, gas masks, etc. Later on Jaramillo met Stanley Hall, and the story repeated another circle when the Scottish explorer renewed his hopes of finding the exact site of the elusive metal library.

WHEN ATAHUALPA
WAS THE KING OF THE INCAS

The "lost treasure" could have been Atahualpa's golden ticket, but one of his generals hid the gold in the Llanganates range, around the same time as Pizarro killed Atahualpa, the king of the Incas. The Llanganates are a dangerous and wild mountain range between the high peaks of the Andes and the Amazon. No one can live there. The land is swampy and deserted, and an eerie feeling penetrates the area (see plate 7). Atahualpa, the lord of the Incas, ruled both countries, Peru and Ecuador. Atahualpa's great grandfather had prophesized that white bearded men would come one day to destroy the Incan Empire.

The chronicles say that one night with a narrow crescent moon was unusually bright, and three rings appeared around it. The first ring was the color of blood, the second was blackish green, and the third one was an almost translucent gray.

On his deathbed, Atahualpa's father, Huayna Capac, told his son to bury his heart in Quito and the rest of his body in Cusco, the heart of the empire. Before his death, he received the prophecy that the empire would fall after the twelfth king.

When Pizarro disembarked in the Ecuadorian coast, Huayna Capac had already died from measles. It is believed this endemic plague came to the colonies from Central America, which was devastated from the conquest in Mexico, or it could have been spread between the Spaniards and natives.

Huayna Capac's complaints were such that his moans rose to the skies, making the birds fall dead on the ground. In Quito they cried for a whole full moon. His body was escorted to Cusco by many chiefs, and the paths were lined by men and women who cried in sorrow, mourning his death. Thousands of wives, assistants, and servants agreed to kill themselves in order to be buried with him.

If the sun god called him in death, the Inca chief could return to Earth. When he came back to life, he could need his earthly possessions. So all the treasure the monarch had accumulated throughout his life would be buried with him, waiting for his return.

Huayna Capac had many sons from different women, but Atahualpa was his favorite, and he fought next to his father in many battles to the north. Before his death, he gave the northern province and its capital, Quito, to his son, while the real heir, his firstborn Huascar (Atahualpa's half brother) would rule the south. This is how the Incan Empire was first divided into north and south. Huascar was more merciful than his brother, who was tough and vengeful.

Since the insurrection continued growing in the north, Huascar sent Atoc, his best general, with forty thousand men to suppress the uprisings. Near Ambato, west of the Llanganates, Atoc was captured and executed. With his skull, which still had pieces of dry skin and hair, they improvised a golden goblet from which they drank his blood and the fermented drink *chicha morada*. They had made a sort of gourd, and through the teeth they stuck the golden straw or bombilla, to drink.

Atahualpa left another half brother in Quito, Ruminyahui, while he left to celebrate his recent victories in the thermal baths of what today is Cajarmarca. Atahualpa went to Quito, knowing Pizarro's men had already disembarked—almost two hundred troops with horses—and even though the Incas had been established as a megaempire for less than a century, they felt invincible.

The Inca army made camp in Cajamarca with over eighty thousand men. This meant they had an advantage of four hundred to one. The messengers from both sides came and went. When the invaders reached Atahualpa's baths, he was gone, and they sent an emissary to agree on a meeting point: Cajamarca.

So Atahualpa went with over six thousand warriors into the city of Cajamarca, which seemed to be deserted. His assistants asked for those who wanted to parlay, when a man wearing black (a priest) stepped into the light to meet them. He had a black book with a golden cross on its cover in his hands. With the help of an interpreter, he started talking to the Incas about the Christian religion. Atahualpa took the Bible, glanced at it, and threw it on the floor. The screams of the priest went above the battle, and it is said that Pizarro screamed, "Let's charge, for Santiago [St. James]!"

The massacre lasted two hours; the streets in the center of Cajamarca were bathed in blood. Spanish swords were sharper than Incan axes. The surprising thing is that not one Spaniard was left dead in the field of the ambush. That same afternoon Atahualpa was taken to the Temple of the Sun, Cajamarca, one of the temples next to his palace. He was still allowed to run his empire from one of the rooms that had been turned into a guarded cell, letting him maintain some privileges of an absolute monarch.

Atahualpa knew and saw that the Spaniards were hungry, and that they went crazy when talking of gold and silver, so he told Pizarro he would fill one of the halls of the temple with treasures in exchange for his freedom. Pizarro made him sign a contract. Atahualpa also sent a messenger to his men and commanded them to maintain their rearguard position. In the meantime, the *chasquis,* royal runners or messengers who used to travel the main roads of the Inca emprire, started spreading the news to the chiefs of the empire in other regions, and they had to make sure they collected the best pieces of gold. This was Atahualpa's error: he told the Spaniards of the existence of other, richer temples like the ones in Cusco or Pachacamac on the northwest coast.

It didn't take long for Pizarro to send his stepbrother Hernando to Pachacamac and another group of men to Cusco. There they captured and destroyed Korikancha, which would be dismantled to become what today is the Dominican Temple of Santo Domingo. By May 1533, the invaders had collected over 1.3 million pesos in gold (the equivalent of $300 million). For over four months, thousands and thousands of artifacts and handicrafts made of solid gold were melted in the improvised campfires in Cajamarca.

Two years later in Spain, King Charles V would order that even the pieces of art that had been taken as presents from the invading expedition were to be melted and turned into ingots in the reserves of Seville, Segovia, and Toledo.

Between the destructive hordes of Pizarro and the king's furnaces, no golden artifact survived, with the exception of the golden frieze that was supposedly in Korikancha. Today it can be found in a museum in Madrid.

4

The Original Discoveries of Juan Moricz

It is said the Tayos Cave was discovered before Juan Moricz's discovery of it in the 1960s. The first description of the caves came from a man called Salvador Festa, an Italian who lived in Ecuador in the nineteenth century. He didn't go inside, but he described the entrance to the Coangos Cave, pointing out its depth.

During the bloody and surreal presidency of Gabriel García Moreno in Ecuador (1861–1875), a precursor of the dictators who would later shape Latin America, there was a general called Proanyo who was confined to eastern Ecuador. There he befriended some Jíbaros who dwelled on the other side of the Upano River. During this period, Proanyo tried to stay in one place and started exploring the surrounding area. He left the Macas region with his Jíbaro friends and started exploring the Upano River area. Proanyo never went down the caves, but it is likely he entered other caves that had easier access from the river.

Some accounts mention Festa, others, General Proanyo, but in our circle, we agree that the real discoverer was Moricz. Geographical and archaeological sites always have countless local stories about people who allegedly have seen them, but the discovery is not acknowledged as such until someone takes possession of the place or records its discovery.

Ecuador is divided into regions and subregions. The Tayos Cave is located in the Amazon-Andean region, meaning the eastern side, which borders the upper Amazon River basin. The coordinates of the Tayos Cave are lat 78°13' W, long 03°05' S; its elevation is approximately 2,556 feet. It is a part of the mountain range of Cutucú and Cóndor, but it does not reach such high elevations. It is surrounded by rivers, and from an explorer's point of view, this makes it interesting but also rather problematic. It is close to the Coangos River, a tributary of the Santiago River. The area is plowed by streams that drain and create picturesque waterfalls. Small rivers multiply here, eroding the inside of the cave, but the products of this erosion must not be confused with the architectonic structures also found inside.

The entrance is almost invisible from the outside; the bushes hide a small and slippery slope that slides almost like a chute toward the dark interior. If you peek over the edge, you can perceive the deep fall; the vertical cave entrance is a couple of feet wide, 229 feet deep, and another 265 feet long after passing through von Däniken's Arch, a well-known stone formation named for author Erich von Däniken in 1976.

JUAN MORICZ: FROM HUNGARY WITH A BIRD ON HIS SHIELD

Though there are alleged sightings that are said to have occurred before his discovery, the story of the Tayos Cave and its mysterious treasures probably begins with Moricz; at any rate, there is no way to tell the story without talking about him. It is also not easy to imagine the wild jungle setting that was Ecuador back then, where fate would keep Moricz until his dying day. You almost feel as if you could see or feel him in certain parts of the suburbs or deep within the Ecuadorian provinces. Without Moricz, the Tayos Cave would never have been revealed. But who was this enigmatic character? Where did he really come from? Why was he here?

We don't know much of Moricz's first years. His claim that he came from a noble famly whose coat of arms showed a bird resembling the oilbird hasn't been proven. Born in 1923 in Hungary and known in Europe as Janos, he became known as Juan only after he moved to South America, a name that stuck with him until his last day. We know he was in the Hungarian army and spent some time in Russian concentration camps. He had shown an interest in multidisciplinary knowledge ever since he was young. His interest in the theories of Hanns Hörbiger and other Nazi scientists who were part of the Thule Society spiked his interest in the subterranean worlds and in traveling to South America.

Nazi theories held that the Andes were a place linked to the gods or demigods that created them. Nazi archaeologists and anthropologists were moved by the large ruins of Tiwanaku in Bolivia and by the monumental constructions of the Incas, such as the ones found around Cusco and in Peru's Sacred Valley of Urubamba.

The inner circle of the Third Reich had a philosophy and had made several plans to search for sacred artifacts, including the Holy Grail. They also searched the sanctuary of the Black Madonna at the Monastery of Montserrat in Catalonia. The Nazis were looking for a contact with a mysterious figure known as the King of the World.

Moricz didn't have to fight because he was considered an Aryan prototype. His allegedly perfect Aryan anatomy gave him a better standing than other Hungarians. It is possible he participated with German scientists in Eastern Europe, not in South America. He got married in France and had a daughter, Veronica, who was missing for a long time but was found recently; apparently she lives in Britain.

According to some sources, the best seller from the sixties *The Twenty-Fifth Hour* was inspired by Moricz's life, because Moricz and the book's author, Orthodox priest Virgil Gheorghiu, had shared prison time together.

Moricz arrived in Argentina after World War II. Julio Goyén Aguado always said he had met Juan Moricz by the late fifties, when he worked as a customs officer. At the time, Moricz was thirty-six years old and Aguado was seventeen. This is how their master-disciple relationship came to be: one wanted to learn, the other needed someone to help him in his search through a country that was new to him.

The first thing Moricz told Aguado was that he was studying the Magyar presence in prehistoric America, thus his interest in the books by Florencio de Basaldúa. This author, of Basque origins, lived in Argentina, and his main theory talked about an Atlantean red race linked to Basque roots. Nineteenth-century authors believed the cradle of that red race was a southern continent (usually known as Lemuria) that disappeared after the last great deluge. The last traces of that race can now be seen in the indigenous population of the Americas, whose roots lay in the prehistoric humans that took refuge in the high peaks of the mountains.

Moricz believed the Magyar had traveled from what is now Eastern Europe and reached America through the Pacific. Agreeing with Basaldúa, he believed the continent of Lemuria served as a land bridge toward what today is the Ecuadorian coast. These two taciturn researchers were connected by their theories, which claimed advanced civilizations from other continents reached America by sea in prehistoric times.

Moricz believed in the existence of a tribe of white indigenous people who dwelled in several places in the Amazon jungle. (A similar belief had led Percy Fawcett to search for these people.) Moricz then started getting interested in the Church of Jesus Christ of Latter-day

Saints (the Mormons) after Aguado told him that its doctrines talked about a white-skinned race in prehistoric Central and South America.

Moricz arrived in Ecuador in 1964 with introduction letters from his Argentinian friends to sell cattle and to interact with historians and intellectuals, mainly in Quito. Andrés Fernández Salvador Zaldumbide remembers him with a certain irony: "I realized he knew nothing of cattle or animals and that he was really looking for something else." His idea was to sell a large number of cattle, which would be transported upriver from Argentina. I looked at the original contracts, which were for thousands of dollars—another financial endeavor in this man's life that would sadly never come to fruition.

It didn't take long for Moricz to reveal his real purpose, which some believed to be naive. "I came to find a subterranean world and kingdom that probably extends from Venezuela to Chile and Argentina," he said.

Moricz believed that fate sent him to the Coangos River. Apparently, during one of his adventures digging for precious minerals and exploring lost cities, Moricz met a witch doctor named Nayambi, who told him of the existence of the caves filled with nests of a bird found on the coat of arms of the Moricz family: the tayo or oilbird, for which Moricz had searched during his first years in Ecuador. These Shuar friends told Moricz that "it was time a white man learned of the reality of the subterranean world." They were speaking of the Tayos Cave. Moricz said, "Some famous caves had been talked about by travelers, but never one of this magnitude, like the Guácharo, which Humboldt visited but didn't disclose the secret of its depth." Jules Verne, in one of his novels, wrongly said the caves' location was in Colombia (and at the time Jules was writing, Colombia was Venezuela). This country, like many other South American countries, has Guácharo Caves.

Moricz spent long days and even weeks inside the cave. How did he orient himself while exploring this lost world? Is there something capable of illuminating that black abyss, which so carefully hides its secrets? Moricz said he entered the Tayos Cave in Ecuador and came out in Peru. He did not say where exactly, but we believe he was telling the truth. His conclusions were sensational, and this thrilled many scientists.

The history of *Homo sapiens* and Cro-Magnon man, from which some of us are descended, does not go back further than 40,000 years, according to strict scientific reasoning. But Moricz asserted that the Tayos Caves were inhabited by the mysterious tribe of the Belas more than 250,000 years ago, and that this tribe was the successor of a superior culture of unknown origin. Moricz also called them the Taltos—immortal beings who might have come from a distant solar system, possibly Ursa Major. They lived in large caves and were protected by a sacred bird that lived in the entrance of these subterranean worlds. There are many caves in the Andes, and quite a few of these are connected to legendary stories about strange beings living inside them.

QUINARA AND THE SPANIARD'S TREASURE

Moricz had had no results in the exhumation or rescue of the treasure of the metallic library, so he decided to do another expedition financed by the Peña Matheus brothers. This time, the expedition was connected to the Quinara treasure. Pio Jaramillo Alvarado spoke of Quinara in his book *History of Loja and Its Province,* and in the area of Vilcabamba there were more recent traces and legends of its existence.

Moricz and the Peña Matheus brothers (Gerardo and Carlos) went for 15 days to Vilcabamba, an area known as the Golden Cross; there they rented a house with a bathroom and a shower. They hired a group of excavators They dug for over 65 feet and found a heart-shaped stone and a series of tombstones called *guajalaches.*

"Juan Moricz used a pendulum and radiesthesia rods . . . but in the end we didn't find anything," Carlos Peña Matheus told me once. They used a system of pulleys that dug out buckets of soil, a standard procedure for archaeological excavations. Peña Matheus noticed the pendulum spun twelve times, clockwise. "Three years after we left, some explorers found an oven used to melt golden bricks, and there is golden sand in the place, where the earth changes and becomes soft. You know, in those places there are higher beings looking over these things, and they also distort your reality. Moricz had good intentions. He wasn't looking for a treasure or for glory, he just wanted to know the truth, and sometimes doors open for you where you can share things that are not seen in plain sight." Moricz said many times that he received messages and orders from the nonvisible beings in the caves that he called the Taltos or Belas. Many people have had strange experiences and visions of beings as well as have taken pictures of cloudy concentrations of vapor taking the shape of phantasmagorical figures.

THE TÁLTOSOK BARLANGJA

After exploring the caves with Aguado, in 1969 Moricz took part in an official civil military expedition with the Ecuadorian Corporation of Tourism (CETURIS). This expedition is also known as the Táltosok Barlangja (*barlang* means *caves* in Magyar). The purpose of the expedition was threefold: (1) find the caves and caverns that hold the artifacts, (2) prove the existence of these artifacts, and (3) inform the truth of the discovery.

Following the 1969 expedition, it didn't take long for Moricz to return to Argentina looking for help from private or official centers. This would lead him to meet Captain Enrique Green Urien and Colonel Carlos María Zavalla, a sociology professor at the University of Buenos Aires. Moricz always tried to get support from

Janos "Juan" Moricz during "Táltosok Barlangja," the first organized civil military expedition in 1969

First official expedition to the Tayos in 1969.
This expedition is the one known as "Táltosok Barlangja."
Here, army soldiers inspect clean cuts of massive blocks.

both countries, Ecuador and his beloved Argentina. Moricz knew it was important to make his discovery public, something he would also do in 1969. His written testimony appears below.

THE NOTARY ACT OF JANOS "JUAN" MORICZ

Register of title in the year 1969 by the 4th notary of the canton of Guayaquil, July 21, 1969

Dear Minister of Finance,

I, Juan Moricz, citizen of Argentina by settlement, born in Hungary, passport number 4361689, by my own right and by your mediation with the office of his Excellency, the President of the Republic, do hereby declare that in the eastern region, in the Province of Morona-Santiago, within the boundaries of the Republic of Ecuador, I discovered valuable objects of great cultural and historical value of mankind. These consist of metal panels that were created by human hand and contain a summary of the history of a lost civilization, of which mankind has currently neither inkling nor proof. I have made this discovery through my own good luck while I was carrying out investigations in my capacity as a scientist specializing in folkloric, ethnological and linguistic aspects of Ecuadorian tribes. The objects I discovered can be described as follows:

1. Objects of various shapes and sizes made of metal and stone.
2. Metal panels engraved with symbols and ideographic scripts.

This is a genuine metal library which contains a summary of the history of mankind; the origin of man on Earth, as well as scientific knowledge about a lost civilization.

The fact of this discovery makes me the legal owner of these objects in concordance with Article 665 of the Civil Code. However, because these are items of immeasurable cultural value and I did not discover them on my own land or property, here applies Article 666 of the Civil Code.

As the land and the caves in which I made the discoveries belong to the State of Ecuador in accordance to Article 55 of today's political constitution, I am required to share my discovery with the aforementioned state. In concordance with the Civil Code, the owners of the land are accorded rights over the discovery.

Therefore, in accordance with the Article 58 of the Constitution of the Republic of Ecuador I have turned to you.

Article 58 states that the artistic and archaeological value of a find remains under control of the State.

In accordance with Articles 3 and 9 of the Agricultural legislation, it is the task of the Finance Ministry to monitor the laws regarding the property of the State, and to inform the President of the Republic.

As a sign of my honesty and willingness to protect the rights of the State of Ecuador, I am registering my discovery with your Excellency, the President of the Republic. I am doing this to ensure that the Republic of Ecuador is in a position to secure both its own and my rights. I would like to request that you set up an Ecuadorian commission of control. I will show this commission the correct and exact position and location of the right caves as well as the objects within. I reserve the right to show the people nominated your photographs, films, and also original drawings.

Furthermore, I would like to state that—in the fulfillment of my rights as the discoverer and owner of this find and in accordance with the law—I will not reveal the very exact location of the find until the members of the commission have been appointed. This commission should also contain members that I may be allowed to appoint.

SEALED AND SIGNED BY PENA MATEUS, ESQ.,
AND JUAN MORICZ OPOS

The lawyer Gerardo Peña Matheus

Gerardo Peña Matheus, Juan Moricz, and Julio Goyén Aguado
at a press conference after Moricz announced his findings
to a notary public in 1969

MORICZ IN THE EYES
OF HIS CONTEMPORARIES

Moricz's story is a legend of survival and courage, as well as of superstition, adaptation to the environment, and transition in Latin American politics that cannot be ignored. Although it is a sad story, it has epic dimensions, with undeniable hints of the supernatural.

Aguado also remembers: "Moricz had an adventurous spirit. He was an adventurer, but an honest one. His objective was to share one of the stories he received with mankind to make known this line of thought about the origin of mankind on the planet. This turned him into a very private and untrusting person."

When Moricz was poor, he had many debts, and people would often come to him to demand that he pay them back. When his situation improved, he believed he needed to do right by the people who had helped him. Many were grieved at his death, because he was a very loyal friend. No one could say he was dishonest or a bad friend.

Descriptions of Moricz may seem ambiguous, but there is no doubt that his reserved personality, his willingness to give his all, and his fear that he would either create or be forgotten led him to fall into silent desperation and oblivion. Moricz was a giant with feet of clay, not without his weaknesses and flaws. Many of his hypotheses bordered on the speculative or fantastic, which led him to be either admired or hated from the ivory tower.

Guillermo Aguirre, the personal biographer of Julio Goyén Aguado, said that Moricz was investigated by the secretary of state intelligence of Argentina, who considered him a con artist. Aguirre also believes many of the important artifacts found their way to Argentina through a Father Arana, a priest who was an early friend of Moricz and Aguardo and who took several of the metallic plates after they had chosen him as their custodian.

Alberto Borges, one of the best journalists in Ecuador and a friend of mine from Guayaquil in the sixties and seventies, thinks that "there is no doubt that Moricz was a remarkable man. It is believed that during World War II he was part of a mysterious German-Hungarian group dedicated to parapsychological phenomena. Then he shows up in Argentina as a speleologist and explores countless caves from Jujuy to the Tierra del Fuego, and later he was spotted in Bolivia and Peru doing geology studies." Moricz has been described as a very private man who almost seemed to have the gift of bilocation—of being in two places at the same time. We need only look at the television show he did in 1976 (on the Guayaquil channel of the Ecuavisa network) to see his passion and conviction.

Héctor Burgos Stone, a Chilean linguist he met close to his death, said Moricz was a real gambler, a man who believed in giving it all or nothing, who loved or hated, who would shut down or light up, who was all passion or all ice. Moricz had a prodigious mind, but his emotional side was damaged; he was a megalomaniac chased by his own paranoia, according to Carlos Peña Matheus, president of Cumbaratza, one of the bigger mines in eastern Ecuador's Oriente region.

Even though Moricz was generous, he was only generous with those he liked. He was surely out of touch with his feelings and emotions, though he knew how to love, how to accept, and how to lose. In many aspects he was a winner, in many others a conscientious loser, like those who fool others by fooling themselves, making themselves believe legends they have heard or read from others.

Other questions are why Moricz stopped talking about the metallic library by the late seventies, even after the pact he made with Aguado to protect the real site of the treasure from the Mormons and the British, and why he was so hostile to those who approached him, like the explorer Stan Grist or the journalistic researcher Andreas Faber-Kaiser.

The story of an ancient, technologically advanced civilization started becoming popular around the sixties and seventies.

Fantastic realism was a literary-philosophical movement originally in France, created by Louis Pauwels and Jacques Bergier with their book *The Morning of the Magicians* and the journal *Planète,* which resounded throughout Spain and even South America. Many of these books, by authors such as Peter Kolosimo and Robert Charroux, would discuss South America in relation to possible influences from both Atlantis and extraterrestrial civilizations. They spoke of a civilization that took refuge in the Andes and left behind a library with information recorded in stone or metal that could bring light to the blurry past of mankind.

Moricz believed these ancient civilizations used insect-shaped machines that roamed the depths of the Earth and connected continents from beneath—a subterranean Gondwana. Moricz did not fully develop his theory, which was connected to other, more orthodox ones, and that was starting to become popular. He believed the origin of cultures took place in the Amazon-Andean region, and from there migrated to Asia Minor. Moricz supported this theory with linguistic theories, mainly based on his experience with the Hungarian language.

Like Moricz, other researchers identified terms similar to Magyar in the Quechua, Aymara, Tupí, and Guaraní languages, as well as in many Brazilian dialects. This is how Moricz managed to communicate with the natives without knowing their language. Moricz believed their ancient ancestors, the Belas, or Taltos, were superior, even if no evidence of their existence had been firmly established.

In their dubious book, *Les Intra Terrestres* Marie-Thérèse Guinchard and Pierre Paolantoni claimed to have interviewed Moricz. They say he confirmed what had been published in the magazines of the seventies. In that interview he said the Taltos, who were short people and whom he identified with the grays (with large, oblique, stretched eyes) that would be known to the world in the late eighties, had many metallic plates.

MORICZ VERSUS CRESPO

Hernán Crespo Toral was an anthropologist and the director of the Museum of the Central Bank of Ecuador, and his meeting with the Hungarian explorer was inevitable. Moricz and Crespo were two illustrious characters who were mortal enemies—one rational, the other irrational; one, a left brain, the other, a right brain.

Crespo never forgave Moricz for speaking with such grandiloquent terms when he "compared the discovery of the caves to the discovery of the Amazon—real nonsense." Crespo would ask me, "So then, where are the artifacts he claims he found? Like the engraved metallic plates that were kept in a large library. If he notified the Directorate of National Heritage of this discovery, what is he waiting for?"

There is no doubt this lack of physical evidence was one of the weakest links of the whole Tayos saga, one I knew about, even after I confirmed it through the testimony of Crespo, a pillar of the Ecuadorian cultural past. I had the opportunity to visit him for the last years of his life; I would visit him after his slow recovery from surgery. I met a brilliant person, who undoubtedly belonged to the classic school of thought of anthropology and culture, in spite of his education in arts and architecture.

Even if I was a skeptic since the beginning, I had to face what I least expected when the team of Father Pedro Porras found remains of a culture that had been inside the cave for eight hundred or one thousand years. Crespo was the official supervisor to Father Porras.

In 1976 Moricz had no other option but to come out of his self-imposed retirement when in Guayaquil, the city he was living in, the memoirs of the Moricz-Táltosok Barlangja Expedition of 1969 were being brought back up.

While Stanley Hall's expedition of 1976 explored the Coangos Cave, Moricz was getting ready to dig out his old hypothesis and come up with some new ones. "You can cross through all of South America underground," Moricz said. He also noted, "I have been in Peru and in the tunnels that communicate with Cusco. In Machu Picchu alone there is one tunnel that reaches the ocean. I don't deny there are natural formations, but there are testimonies of monumental constructions made by man, used as shelter from cataclysms."

MORICZ'S THEORIES

Jules Verne used Alexander von Humboldt's explorations as inspiration for the classic book, beloved by all those who are passionate for the subterranean world, *Journey to the Center of the Earth*. This novel would definitely have an influence on Moricz. Beyond exploring the caves, Moricz was interested in many aspects of prehistory.

The treasure of Atahualpa, last emperor of the Incas, was also a recurring theme for Moricz, who sometimes linked it to the Tayos. The tomb of Atahualpa was never found, but a legend says that a relative of Atahualpa took his wife through open rock passageways to subterranean gardens. Here they walked through trees and animals represented in pure gold, as was the king's palanquin. It has

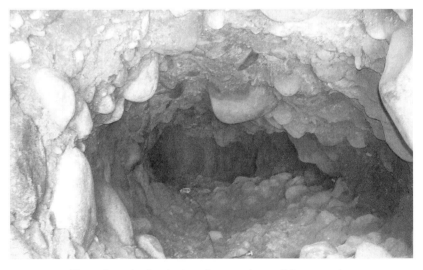

Tunnel to Atahualpa's palace and possible gravesite

been said that the remains of the emperor were in the Tingo María Cave, where the famous Lechuza Cave was located, and this is why no one dared go inside.

When Moricz was asked about the Nazca lines, or sun-oriented paths, he said, "They are a part of the immense picture of a lost civilization. Nazca was an exterior sign, but there are other signs. Just 6.2 miles from the entrance to one of the Tayos Caves, there are several rocks placed in a special position. The stones show ideograms and low-relief figures with instructions. I made this discovery not long ago, from what I found in the caves. I followed the inner path, but if I had found those stones before, the task would have been much easier." Between 1964 and 1968 Moricz made explorations following his insight and intuition, but he was also showing signs of being a treasure hunter and gold seeker.

I found this statement by Moricz in the journal *El Telégrafo* from Guayaquil, thanks to the Argentinian journalist Jorge Blinkhorn: "The subterranean world exists, and in its chambers I have found objects and archives of great historical and cultural importance for mankind." Moricz believed that the *turul* birds were "sacred birds of the seven hordes" of the Scythian and Magyar nations. *Turul* is the name of a Hungarian bird, but also the name of the main plaza in Sígsig, in the Azuay Province of Ecuador. Moricz was interested in connections between Magyar, the ancient language of his native Hungary, and languages of the natives of South America. Similarities between words and place names drew his attention.

Moricz already had many theories forming when he lived in Buenos Aires. Later he would take these with him to Guayaquil, serving as a self-proclaimed master for young Ecuadorians, who were impressed by his physical and intellectual stature.

With a strong, almost supernatural conviction, Moricz developed and dispersed a tale of a library of metallic books that told of the history and scientific knowledge of an unknown advanced civilization.

Juan Moricz on horseback

This hidden civilization of the sacred subterranean world of the Andes was said to speak ancient Magyar, the mother tongue of the Cara, Maya, Euskara, Quechua, Sumerian, Sanskrit, and other languages. He believed there were some ancestors connected to Atlantis who called themselves "Antis." He developed an early hypothesis of a relation between the Huns and South America, a view revised through the work of Father Gregorio García.

For over two hundred years it has been said the barbarians from the East traveled great distances to the West and reached the Americas as well as Europe. Reinhold Forster, in his book *History of the Voyages and Discoveries Made in the North,* suggests that the real founders of the pre-Columbian kingdoms of Peru and Mexico were descendants of troops sent by Kublai Khan to conquer Japan.

On a television show, Moricz declared that the metallic library had extraterrestrial origins and that it belonged to the first culture to inhabit the zone, the Atlanteans, who had a mainly Magyar language and had come from Ursa Major. I have confirmed that, like other ancient peoples such as the Egyptians, many Andean cultures, especially the pyramid and *huaca* (monument) builders in the Ecuadorian coast and mountains, oriented their structures toward Ursa Major and Ursa Minor, as I witnessed at the site of the Cochasquí pyramids north of Quito.

Moricz believed that after the universal deluge, or the Great Flood, the Americas became, or were reborn as, the "Mother of Ancient Civilization." Atlantean theories of dispersion and transmigration describe that groups of humans took refuge in the Andes, 9,850 feet above sea level, and after surviving they descended to the valleys and dispersed thousands of miles over continents and across oceans.

Between 8000 and 7000 BCE they arrived in Lower Mesopotamia using totara and balsa tree rafts to get to such places as Shumir, Zumir, and Mosul. They also traveled to Shamar in the Ecuadorian region of Azuay.

Ecuadorian and other Andean people, especially around the Amazon basin, share the same languages and words in addition to sharing legends and myths, many of them predating the deluge. This is why Moricz started studying which aboriginal groups spoke ancient Magyar, such as the Salasakas, Cayapas, Tschachis, and Shuar. Shared words and phrases such as Nap, "sunlight"; Ur, "mister"; and Isten, "god"; are not mere coincidences.

At the end of the eighth century CE, a specific Magyar group who would evolve into the Karas (a name that coincides with the white Huns) migrated from Hindustan to South America. According to Father Juan de Velasco, the Karas (or Caras) arrived at a bay that today is Manabi in Ecuador.

Experts believe the Magyar language may have had a musical

perfection; perhaps it was organized by a mathematical code. The mystery of the Hungarian language is a divine secret that could shine a light on many ethnographic and archaeological enigmas. Magyar is one of the most ancient languages, and it is also one of the most advanced and elaborate, like Sumerian and Egyptian.

Sumerians wrote in pictographs and pictograms called cuneiform, much like the Egyptians, who used simplified figures and effigies shaped like lettered symbols that would develop into hieroglyphs.

The relationship between the alphabet and the Sumerian writing was connected to the Glozel Stones, which in turn were connected to Atlantis, since the stones date back to 10,000 BCE. The names inscribed in them, such as Funotian, Funo, Huno, Hunnotian, Fenice, and Funno, are connected to the prehistory of the Huns and Magyars, as well as to the South American Andes, the Anteans, and the Atl-Anteans, because they show a correlation between how the word sounds and what it means. The Phoenician alphabet is considered one of the nearly perfect ones from ancient times. It was influenced by proto-alphabets and other alphabets were born from Phoenician, like Hebrew, especially biblical Hebrew.

The most ancient Hebrew inscription is in the Moabite Stone (900 BCE), which is written in Hebrew, but with Phoenician characters. The Hebrew letters recognized actually belong to the Aramaic alphabet, one of the oldest languages that connects Magyar, Basque, and other languages of the Andes with the mystery of the connection to the diaspora of Hebrew.

Comparative charts leave no doubt of the connection between prehistoric and protohistoric cultures from Europe, such as the Iberian and Azilian alphabets, with the Numidian and Berber, regions that were connected to the Masmudas (Masmas).

Despite much analytical research and actual exploration, the main characters in the saga of the Tayos did not leave behind many written testimonies, even if the discovery of these caves have a unique and complex nature that is deserving of a monumental book.

This has always perplexed me. I remember when my friend Aguado sent me a book about the forgotten tenor Florencio Constantino to see if another acquaintance of mine, Plácido Domingo, would agree to share some words of support during the book launch, which would take place at the Colon Theater in Buenos Aires. Aguado's book was monumental—the perfect coffee-table book, including many illustrations and unique photographs. I couldn't help but wonder why Aguado would publish such a book when his most important task was speleological exploration and when the expeditions to the Tayos Caves deserved something as grand as the monumental book he was working on. There are only a few pages left of Aguado's personal travel journal, mainly from the time of the Mormon expedition.

Another mystery is that Moricz never really published any extensive material in his life, not even about the Tayos. As an explorer and scholar, he only published texts about the cultural connections between the New and Old Worlds. As you will see here, ancient texts, written mostly by Jesuit chroniclers, explained the theory that Ecuadorians descended from Hungarian and Mongolian slaves— barbarians from the East—who had arrived from Eurasia to the South American Andes.

Here, translated and edited for the first time in English, is the transcription of Moricz's revealing essay under the title, "The American Origin of European Civilization."

THE AMERICAN ORIGIN OF EUROPEAN CIVILIZATION ACCORDING TO JUAN MORICZ

Every Story Begins in Sumeria

The exclusion of the American continent from the cultural and historical movement of civilizations is the cornerstone of the distortion reflected by our current knowledge of prehistory.

The complex issues behind the origin of civilization and cultures cannot be solved because the American continent has been excluded from our globe. In our planet, prehistoric civilizations made many travels; they moved, formed, and diffused our current cultural heritage.

Thus current researches on our prehistory have a lack of global vision of the civilizations that intervened in the formation and diffusion of our history.

The confusion around this topic grows worse as we study other disciplines, each one of which daily announces new discoveries. Today a good archaeologist must discover at least one or two new cultures. In this wild race they are only searching for vases, plates, and so on to find new hints of cooking, color, engraving, prints, polishing, or a new horizon or time of some of the already classified cultures.

This is how we have come to record hundreds of cultures in relatively small areas. No one would dare say two cars were produced by two different cultures, one built on our continent with the engine in the front, and the other manufactured on the other side of the globe, with the engine in the back.

This would be like mixing up the style of Louis XIV with the style of two different cultures, and this happens nowadays.

Linguistic research is doing no better. For the American continent there are 396 classified languages, arbitrarily divided in groups and subgroups. Thus in the linguistic map we find little-known regions in the Amazon that harbor a large array of different languages in a very small area, so that it seems that a different language is spoken under each tree.

Regarding the supposed arrival of men to the American

continent, there is a surprising general agreement on the migration theories of the Bering Strait.

Cultural Unity

The American continent has a fascinating cultural unity that extends to Polynesia, Melanesia, and Micronesia. It goes further along the equator all the way to India and lower Mesopotamia, and then on to Central Europe and the Iberian peninsula.

Mankind wrote its history along this line, which follows the path of the sun. As we move farther north and south, we see fewer and fewer large cultural hubs.

That same path of the sun was used by the ancient inhabitants of America for their large ocean migrations. Every ancient tribe could see the same constellations along the latitude of the equatorial line, and by day they all sailed following the path of the sun.

Their extraordinary knowledge of the four basic elements—earth, water, air, and fire—is evident because the American continent is the only one with temples built for each one of them, which confirms the cultural unity of the prehistoric cultures of the continent. Two of the temples are located in the southern hemisphere and two in the northern hemisphere.

Transoceanic trips, even if they took a long time, were common feats thanks to the knowledge of the tides and winds, as well as the precious tools they used to sail, such as balsa poles.

American cultures have a rich marine tradition that is embedded in their oral traditions, and until recently they still made long trips on rafts along the Pacific coasts, from Tumbes in Peru and Guayaquil in Ecuador to Panama and Mexico, and carried loads of over one hundred tons.

They demonstrated great mastery of ships suitable for transoceanic travels.

So far these cultures have not given us any clues that would lead us to believe they crossed the frozen ice floes of the Bering Strait to reach America; if they had, they would surely have left behind indelible evidence in their traditions and legends.

Of course, even today an expedition of this magnitude, using the necessary equipment and knowing where the journey will end, is a feat worthy of admiration.

Cultural Diffusion from America

Today it is important to give the American continent the place it is due in the history of the migration of the cultures, recognizing its part in our cultural heritage.

The high peaks of the Andes are practically inaccessible today because of the lack of oxygen in the area, but they are the home of an extraordinary culture that flourished and cultivated the land, a remarkable civilization that survived the fateful days of the universal deluge in the cities and fortresses that crown the high peaks of the Andes.

Groups of humans survived in other areas of the planet, but the antediluvian culture found shelter in the American continent, as shown by its later diffusion.

In 8000 to 7000 BC an Andean civilization, sailing on rafts, reached and settled lower Mesopotamia. They later spread out and were absorbed by other cultures, which in turn passed on the acquired knowledge.

This culture has been called Sumir, Shumir, or Sumer. They are reckoned as the first humans because they learned ideographic writing and later cuneiform writing. Their cradle has not yet been found, and as so often happens, their origin is attributed to the great Asian deserts, where all medieval tales place the origin of civilization.

The Sumer culture originated in America, and from this continent they sailed to lower Mesopotamia. In the provinces of Azuay, Cañar, and Loja in Ecuador, many names still subsist related to the Sumer, Zumer, Shumir, Sumir, and Zhumir.

In the north of Peru, in the department of Libertad, there is a city in ruins covered by desert sand: Chan Chan. It covers an area of approximately 12.5 square miles. In spite of the time gone by and the ravages of time and men, the ancient city with its irrigation channels and decorated city walls that still stand are an example of an urban planning that we often fail to see in our modern cities.

Chan Chan and its culture survived with the Sumerians. Their extraordinary ornamental richness, ceramics, golden embossing in their jewels; their tombs, seals, and painting; their urban planning; and their concept of life are faithfully reflected in lower Mesopotamia.

The Two Progenitors: The Magyars
In India, lower Mesopotamia, Asia, and Europe are many cultures that originated on the [South] American continent, from which some migrated thousands of years ago. In this new environment, they grew apart from their linguistic and racial roots, but others who left more recently still keep their American languages and traditions.

One of these cultures is the Magyar, which today can be found in Europe in the Carpathian basin. The Magyar go back to only two progenitors—Gog and Magog*— and their traditions place the ancestral father sun in the

---

*Gog and Magog are mentioned in the Bible in Ezekiel 38:2.—*Ed.*

center of the world. This tradition was still present in the city of Quito, which called itself the "center of the world," and its name preserves the tradition of its progenitors, because its story goes back to the ancient kingdom of Kitus, which in the Magyar languages means *two progenitors*: *kid = two*, *us = progenitors*. In present-day Magyar it would be *ket-os*.

Guayaquil, one of the largest cities in Ecuador, keeps a beautiful and meaningful memory in its name. The correct etymology of its ancient name, *Uaya*, is from: *u = ancient, ancestral*; *aya = mother*, in ancient Magyar. Thus its meaning is *ancestral* or *ancient mother*. In current Magyar it corresponds to *o-anya*.

Toponyms and patronyms in America still keep their ancient Magyar denominations. This is more evident in the regions where the original names are still preserved, such as Bolivia, Chile, Peru, Ecuador, Colombia, Venezuela, and Mexico, but in an in-depth study, we would be able to connect *Ushuaia* to the Bering Strait.

The famous captain Quisquis, who fought the Spaniards, had a purely Magyar name, in spite of phonetic distortions: *quisquis = kis = small* or *little*. This would be *kis-k* in modern Magyar.

The name of the capital of the Incan empire, Cusco, corresponds to the province of Veszprem in Hungary, which is written indistinctly *Usko* or *Osko*, and means *us = os = ancestral* and *cu = ko = stone*; hence, *ancient stone*.

Today in Ecuador there are autochthonous cultures that speak ancient Magyar, such as the "colored Indians" from Santo Domingo de los Colorados. This tribe, although it is close to a highway that connects Quito to Guayaquil, has kept its traditions and ancient language intact.

The Cayapas too, who live next to the Santiago, Cayapas, and Onzole Rivers, keep their Magyar language, like all groups that live far away from civilization, in the eastern foothills of the mountain range and the Andes.

The ancient Magyar language still spoken today in America is easier to understand for those who know the Magyar that existed before the linguistic reforms of the beginning of the [twentieth] century, or for those who lived in Hungary, where the vowel *u* is still used instead of *o* and *i* instead of *e,* and so on.

The ancient American toponyms and patronyms are found all over India, lower Mesopotamia, and especially Hungary. They were disseminated in these areas by transoceanic migrations, as happened with the Spanish language, which today covers almost all the American continent, and which was introduced in the continent by a maritime route.

In India there were always large hubs of Magyar populations, and they constantly kept in touch with the American continent, as remembered by the annals of India: the Puranas, Rigveda, Avestas, and so on. These Magyar hubs are usually called White Huns, or Kunos, Hephtalites, Sakas, or Kmer. Even in the eighth century CE a large part of India went back to being a kingdom of the White Huns.

Of Basques and Mayas

This is the reason Magyar researchers focused their attention on India, where they spent all their efforts but never found the origin of their culture and were overwhelmed by the mysterious appearance and disappearance of cultures that appeared out of nowhere, or disappeared without leaving a trace.

The Basque researchers have followed this same process to trace their heritage back to India but never have elucidated their origin, which is also American.

The Basques belong to the same racial and linguistic branch as the Huns.

In the final stages of the eighth century CE, a Magyar tribe, the Karas, which were royal Escites, returned to India and prepared a fleet that sailed to return to the ancient motherland of the Magyar.

The mysterious disappearance of the Karas worried researchers for years. They knew if they found this tribe, they would solve the problem of Magyar origins, because they returned to their motherland.

In 1965, as I continued studying prehistory, I arrived in Ecuador, where I learned that one of the biggest conundrums that worried Ecuadorian historians and researchers was the mysterious arrival by sea of the Kara tribe by the end of the eighth century CE, verified in Caraquez Bay in Manabi province.

One of the biggest mysteries the arrival of the "Karas" posed was the introduction of the vowel *o*, according to historian Juan de Velazco, because before then they didn't know it and used the *u*, as still happens in many regions of Hungary.

Juan de Velazco (1727–1792): History of the Ancient Kingdom of Quito

The annals of India narrate in great detail that the Kunos come from America, where they traveled often by sea.

Certain annals say Bappa [a royal Hun with similar names found in the Pacific], aware that he had left the foundations for his dynasty, returned to Transoceania, to the land of his forefathers, Kanisha and Kamaksen, the true land of the Scythian Khomanos (Kunos—Magyar).

The autochthonous population of Colombia is purely *kun,* meaning the ancient inhabitants of Colombia are the Scythian Kunos.

The annals of India, aside from mentioning the Maya, state that these are excellent builders who arrived in Transoceania. The ancient cities of Mohenjo-Daro and Harappa in India [Pakistan] are irrefutable proof of this.

No researches on prehistory have been done because, aside from excluding the American continent from the cultural unity and diffusion on Earth, they also extracted the oral traditions and legends of the tribes, claiming these were just nonscientific creations.

An example of this is the story of Schliemann, discoverer of Troy, using the oral traditions compiled by Homer. His theories were marked as fantasies. This is why we have been stuck, and many Magyar tribes that have a real ancient history told in their mythology would have found the origin of their cultures if people had paid more attention to their traditions, which their elders kept for centuries.*

I have often confirmed that research that seems to be scientific is in fact not at all related to reality or to the real events that took place.

A very sad and unfortunate episode casts a shadow over the Spanish conquest of America. The Spanish Crown knew for some time of the historic truth of America, but, probably for political reasons, they stopped the revelation of the real findings of Christopher Columbus.

---

*As an example of a text that recalls these traditions, Moricz cited Arnold Ipolyi, *Magyar Mythology* (Budapest, 1853). *Codex Epistolarium Monuments Hungariae Historica:* Scriptorium XXV (National Library Budapest, 1875).

Once the Spanish Crown had secured its control, it closed off the borders of the New World and took to the task of erasing the linguistic and cultural traces found in it, in turn promoting the idea of the New World. This political fact is confusing still today and distorts reality, blurring the vision of researchers.

When Spanish researchers do a more in-depth study of the Iberian civilization, which gave its name to the peninsula they now live in, they will find that they are descendants of American tribes, and the confusion and destruction they did in America they did to their own ancestors.

Even if they try to hide it, in America there are precious documents that serve as evidence of these statements.

The Diocesan Synod of Quito

In 1593, there was a synod presided over by Brother Luis López Solís. Only sixty years after the arrival of Benalcazar to Quito, he said: "Experience has taught us that in our district there is a diversity of languages that are not found in Cusco and Aymara, and in order to bring Christianity to them, it is important we translate the catechism and the confessional into their own languages."

The corresponding translations were made, but the Christian faith was never propagated in these languages, which were different dialects of the Magyar language. On the contrary, when the Spanish Crown heard of this laudable initiative, Brother López ordered a linguistic modification, which was inexorably complied with, as evidenced in the Royal Letters of Orders and Decrees.

At the end of the seventeenth century, Puruhá (Magyar) was a living language, because in 1691 it had to be used, by royal decree, over the teaching of Spanish and "in the places where not even the Inca language is spoken, and only their mother Puruha tongue is spoken, more effort must be done, even punishment, for those who do not speak Spanish."

Chronicler from the Indies

During the conquests of the Indies, many eyewitnesses tried to share the events and the real facts of what happened during the Spanish conquest of the American continent. One of these was a Brother Gregorio, who lived for many years among the sugarcane plantations in Ecuador. It is surprising that if he was dedicated to research into the languages of the indigenous populations of the area, he wrote no more than a few words about the place he knew so well.

In the 1729 edition of Brother Gregorio's book, the reader is told that certain changes were implemented to improve the work, because there were doubts surrounding this extraordinary text, which gave the impression that the church censored what they did not want to be known.

Nevertheless, his work is worthy of study, and I will quote some passages that will help us understand more about the Huns, the Kunos, and the Magyars, which are autochthonous cultures from America and were very well known to this priest.

Fourth Book, Chapter XI: About the Scythians and other nations that descended from them who populated the West Indies from the north and east

The first reason behind this assumption is the incredible multitude of Huns, whose names propagated in the conquered nations. They came to have 103 hordes or clans, which at first were only seven. This was the reason why Nikephoros Kallistos called them *Chagano*, "King of Seven People, Seven Weathers, or Regions."

They spoke Magyar. Cedreno calls Moageres the brother of Gordas, king of the Huns of Bosporan, who arose with the kingdom.

The Tartars were said to have the same origin as the Scythians, in seven lineages, hordes, or clans from which they all descended, and who disseminated in Europe and were the last Scythians, according to Krantzio. Like those who moved to the East, called Magores, they were not that much different from the Magiaros or Huns, and their proper names are similar, as Hornio says.

Fourth Book, Chapter XII: About the time the Huns and Scythians traveled to the East and West Indies

The Huns, Avars, Tartars, Mongolians, and Parthians, and other nations mixed with the Huns, made a recent and numerous entrance. They seem to have inhabited the farthest coasts of Asia, near the Mongolian Empire. In the provinces of Cunad and Ung the dwellers are called Huns, Cunads, or Cunadians, as they were called in Hungary.

The name Funotian, if spoken softly, sounds like Hunotian. Unchia is similar to the name Tuchan, the neighboring tribe of Quivira. The Huyrons, Scythians mentioned by Vicente Bellovacente, are undoubtedly the Hurons, Indians of the Five Nations of Canada, whose main tribe was the Carragouiba. The Umitasaston tribe of the Neutras Indians begins with the name of the Huns.

The name of the Uros, who were a very wild tribe, according to Garcilaso, is a clear corruption of the name *Huns*;

they were so happy with their name that if someone asked them if they were men, they would answer that no, they were Uros. The same thing happened with the Chuchos and Contales: they seem to be mixed Chinese and Alans, like the Hungarians.

Unitan, in Brazilian, is a name imposed by the Huns that populated this land through the Magellan Strait, and the Five Nations of the Ennos Indians are in it, the Huns.

The Hipice Ierva [herb] that Pliny describes—and it is doubtful whether this is the same plant Theophrastus mentions in his *History of Plants*—was used by the Scythians, who would put it in their mouths and would not feel hunger or thirst for twenty-eight hours. They would have it with some mare's-milk cheese for twelve days. This is a mixture they called *Hipace,* or the heaviest from the mare's milk, and they drank it in wooden glasses. The foam they called *lard,* according to Hippocrates. His contemporary Herodotus states more clearly: "The Alima Ierva is said to also take away hunger"—the use the indigenous people gave to coca and other chewable herbs.

The Huns were also described by ancient chronicles as "short, deformed, and wild-looking, with yellow, flat, and beardless faces. The weird shapes and incomprehensible language repelled the Latin people. *Where were they coming from?* Popular belief has named them the sons of countries from the other side of the world."

Their feats were constantly told in Chinese chronicles. "They made brief and terrible appearances in dynasty life, and historians attributed a mysterious origin to these strange beings that came from Kuei-Fong, or the Country of the Spirits. Their race was divided into numerous independent tribes; the most important one was ruled by an ancient imperial family that lived on the plateau of the Danube river valley.

Our Cultural Heritage

The generous cultural contribution of America to the world, which today is diffused throughout the globe, and which laid the foundations for the development of our civilization, must not continue to go unrecognized.

Political reasons are not good enough any more. Even if they represent the truth of a civilization, a dynasty, or kingdom in the past, today the truth of the way in which these tribes forged our history and gave us our cultural heritage must prevail above all.

Men have now looked up to the stars, but they must not forget about the small planet they live on, which has been the setting of the fights, blood, and fires that wrote human history.

This story must be known by the people of the world, and the sun that illuminated the path of the brave American tribes will shine more the day the people of the world witness these majestic peaks of the Andes Mountain range, the ancestral homeland where the culture we all inherited was born.

JUAN MORICZ,
BUENOS AIRES, JULY 1967

5

The Intraterrestrial Atlanteans

*The key to the mystery of Ancient South America—
and maybe Prehistory—will be found if we locate those
ancient cities of the Solar Civilization.*

COLONEL PERCY FAWCETT, CA. 1925

Moricz worked his whole life to find evidence of an intraterrestrial civilization. Since he arrived in South America, the Hungarian explorer had more than one ace up his sleeve, although some were very far up his sleeve. His search for the Atlanteans became entangled with the search for extraterrestrials. This was an innovation in every sense. Moricz's explorations went ahead of von Däniken's hypotheses, which would see the light in 1968, with the publication of *Chariots of the Gods? Memories of the Future—Unsolved Mysteries of the Past.*

With the help of many of Moricz's contemporaries and friends, I discovered that he wanted to prove that extraterrestrial beings had influenced primitive South American tribes. But he also wanted to prove a connection between the Americas and the Old World. He was not only after the Magyar cosmovision, which he believed was forgotten in the darkness of the Altai region and the sub-Siberian tundra; he was after evidence of a culture that came from the stars.

Moricz's search was a continuation of a European movement that wanted to acquire power and higher awareness by finding the sources of a lost civilization. The Nazis had found this in the Gate of the Sun in Tiwanaku, Bolivia. This is why they tried to organize an expedition, with about twenty men, to go places no human had ever been before. It may be why Moricz wound up in Argentina and later in Ecuador in the first place.

Moricz's theories followed this line of thought through and through, but he had no idea that the more he talked about his discoveries, the more he was becoming a conspirator against his own reputation. Moricz was afraid throughout his life. He felt a fear, almost paranoia, of being slandered, as he proved when he tried to open up and share his inner beliefs and experiences of the fantastic with the outer world. Introverted and taciturn, he gave no interviews, and after the English expedition of 1976, he closed himself off to the world more and more. He even kept away from those close to him, such as the Peña Matheus brothers and Aguado. He tried to stay away from that topic that had made him a protagonist of two worlds: reality and the unproven fantastic world.

Even so, his privacy in peaceful Guayaquil would be invaded by two French authors, who had been lured by von Däniken's work. This happened in the late seventies, when the world had just experienced one of the largest UFO waves in history (1977–78).

THE FRENCH DISTORTION

Over forty years ago, two French researchers, Marie-Thérèse Guinchard and Pierre Paolantoni, interviewed Moricz and wrote down his experiences in a bizarre book, *Les Intra Terrestres*.

Moricz appears in the French book under the pseudonym "Yan," whom they describe as "a Hungarian archaeologist who came directly from his home country to find more about the fabulous treasure of Atahualpa, the vanquished Inca who was betrayed and murdered by the hordes of Spaniards of the sixteenth century." Here are some transcribed fragments from their interview with Moricz, translated into English:

I have been studying the virgin jungles and the mountain range, with only my backpack, for about twenty years. I have walked through Inca paths that still have traces left. I have lived with indigenous tribes, and I have slowly come to the conclusion that one of these tribes has the secret, the key to the mystery.

One day I came across the Jíbaros, head shrinkers. . . . As you know I am Hungarian, but strangely enough, I could understand their language. I was surprised to discover they have ancient Magyar roots, which I know well. This made my communication with them easier, and even if they had a reputation for violence, they were very friendly to me. I was intrigued, so I lived with them for two months, but not for one second did I believe they could be the ones holding the secret. . . .

The people in the tribe I lived with had all the same tattoos on their cheeks and chin. One day I was with two of them, and we walked too far away from the tribe, so we had to camp in a peaceful area. When we got to this place, we found two other Jíbaros. I didn't believe this encounter was normal, and I found it even weirder that these two Jíbaros were sitting atop a giant rock engraved with the same sign of their tattoos. I thought the engraving was very ancient. What did this sign mean? I asked my friends because I fully trusted them. . . .

The vegetation was hiding an entrance to a cave. The rock marked the exact spot. I came close to the edge of the entrance, which was barely three feet wide, two maybe, and it opened over a chimney that was seven to thirty-two feet deep. I leaned in and saw a lateral opening carved on the rock. Ten minutes later, we had woven a rope from vines, and we went down into the semidarkness of the abyss. Equipped with my magical lantern, I dived in to this mysterious corridor. In the middle, an immense column, maybe made of quartz or crystal, captured the light on the floor and distributed it inwards. Suddenly, the gallery bent in a right angle after a curve in the other direction, and we entered a circular room. In the middle there was a round stone-carved table with seven seats also made from stone. I noticed seven rectangular openings on the rock behind them. Seven doors! In front of each one of them was a seat.

I retraced my steps, realizing the scope of my discovery. I decided to do everything I could to explore in depth the city under the Andes, but with the necessary materials and equipment for an undertaking of such nature. . . .

It took me a month to go back to the city. I told my friends of the fantastic discovery and explained the urgent need to organize an expedition, with food, portable lights, weapons, etc. The cost of operation, the difficult access, and the known and unknown dangers had all those I trusted hesitating. I was desperately in front of the door to the unknown without being able to walk in when José [the lawyer] agreed to help me. We estimated the cost of the expedition, and thanks to him we managed to get the money. To keep the ownership of my findings, I had to make it official. Without expecting more than just moral support, I asked an audience with the Ministers of Culture and Tourism.

The discovery of an underground civilization would not be officially published until I had irrefutable, palpable evidence of its existence, for example, with objects, documents, or photographs to verify the authenticity of my tale. Only then would the authorities organize a new expedition. The Minister of Culture told me the discovery would be mine, but not the caves, because since they were in their territory it was up to their government to decide how to exploit them. He acknowledged I would be fully compensated. Deep down he didn't believe me, but he didn't want to take the chance to pass on what could mean a fortune for the state. His representative insisted that the operation had to be organized with the utmost discretion, without attracting the attention of their powerful neighboring country and yellow journalists.

After ten days of walking through the jungle with the lawyer, Moricz arrived at the Jíbaro lands with his friends. There he interviewed the chief of the village and asked him to please let his son, Genaro, guide him to the caverns, as he had the last time.

The old man's pride gave in to the memory of his ancestors, who would find his son a coward compared to me, because I was willing to risk my life to find the subterranean civilization. He warned us of the dangers we would face, and told us the story of the intraterrestrials, just as he learned from his father before him.

The inhabitants of the caverns are gods, he said, they have dominated the strength of the earth and the sun. They have lightning that kills, with which you can pierce through mountains. Their kingdom extends under the roots of the virgin jungle. When my father was hunting, he saw the earth open and a bright star rise to the heavens. You will never reach the place if the shadows that inhabit it do not want you to.

The old man looked into my eyes and placed his two hands on my chest. Only you will be able to hear their voices. Only you know the language of our fathers. But be careful with what your eyes will see. You will not be able to stand the brightness of the metal shining like fire. You must touch nothing. You must take nothing, not even an atom of that fire metal; even if you believe you are alone, their eyes will follow you wherever you go.

We used a ladder to go down the slippery walls covered by droppings of the night birds that inhabit the vertical hole. With the help of our two armed guards and the Jíbaros we used picks and shovels to clean a few feet of the hall in no time. We did not see any trace of cement, yet the stones were tightly fitted together.

José, a guard, and I retraced the path I walked the first time, which took me to that illuminated first room . . . through the crystal column. A disc covering the surface of the ceiling was drawn over our heads, a light disc, with a weak clarity that slowly invaded the whole space of the cave. . . . It was not sunlight, but a sort of sweet phosphorescence that bathed the giant room, leaving no shadows around. . . . What clever ingenuity created such luminous flux? . . .

We suddenly heard a roaring stream, and water started filling up the gallery . . . the water was covering the exit. I decided to walk through the water . . . and when I went through the wall of water I found myself on a small hill over which the water was falling. I could see a giant cavern opening over a virgin jungle . . . measuring approximately sixty-six feet wide and thirty long. The maximum height was maybe between thirty-three and forty-nine feet. Following the course of the cascade we went down to the lowest part of the cavern. . . .

Under our feet, through the water flowing from the main cascade, I saw polished stones, worn out by water erosion. These were slabs that drew a path to the edges of the cavern forest. We held our hands because we feared we would fall into the abyss, and we walked together through the narrow door into a minuscule hall that went deep into the mountain. Blinded by gusts of wind and water, I looked for support with my hands on the ground to distract myself from the worrisome sensation of not walking on solid ground. . . .

I rummaged through the wet soil, and four inches deep my finger touched rock. It was flat and smooth . . . they looked like slabs and we slid inwards with difficulty. . . . One after another, we went down a stairway of similar steps; it was an endless stairway. The light from my lamp was now weaker and getting lost in the shadows, finding no obstacles. . . . At the foot of the stairway we started walking horizontally. We found ourselves in a gallery with no apparent construction. The ground was made of soil. The gray rock of the stairway was black and shiny. It was not obsidian, but it was so polished that the light from our lamps reflected on some places. . . .

After more than one mile of silent marching, we turned west, where the gallery descended through gentle slopes. We had been walking for about an hour when we reached a dark cave. We were disappointed to see there was no workmanship in this cavity, and the ceiling was too low . . . it also had a small lake in the middle, but no flowing water . . . this time we reached a dead end. . . .

We went back into the cave we had left hours earlier. Our

lamps lit up the big hole. The lake had dried . . . after the wall there was another room where the sounds, which didn't resemble any natural phenomenon, came from. . . . There were high and low modulations, which could only be emitted by animals or human beings.

Just six feet away a door opened, leading to a platform. I hadn't seen it before! We had to figure out if the cave being filled by water, and the lake with it, was a natural phenomenon or if it was caused by human hands. If it was the product of human hands, it was clear someone tried to eliminate us, but now they were opening the path for us. Were they sending us to new traps? Had we finally won the right to enter the forbidden city? . . .

In the darkness three figures appeared to my right and three to my left. . . . They had human forms, and were shorter than the average person. Their heads were long and narrow toward the skull. Were they wearing some sort of helmet? . . .

Walking around in the shadows, I discovered a large gate with columns in the entrance of a gallery. We felt a curious need to walk over a moving light beam. The source of the light came from deep within the cavern. It was a sort of rotating mirror projecting its beams toward me.

I walked into the center of the room . . . all around me and as far as the eye could see I saw a mountain of shining gold. Under my feet and all around me I spotted human skeletons, immobilized in the most natural positions, completely covered by a thin layer of gold. Masks, necklaces, and bracelets adorned those who were most likely the high dignitaries of this mysterious civilization. . . .

In the middle of the cavern with a ceiling that reminded me of a moonless and starless night, I saw a desk of polished

stone. Over it, there were large open books with golden
pages. . . . I barely dared to brush the golden pages with
engraved hieroglyphs. . . .

I suddenly found myself again surrounded by darkness. The light had disappeared. There was a perfume that
reminded me of incense around me. Time had stopped . . .
a distant shining light slowly illuminated a podium . . .
I could see four silhouettes. They were short men dressed
with long gowns or capes made of a fabric that sparkled
under the light. Were these metallic gowns or fabrics with
woven golden threads? Each one of them had a silver tri-
angle hanging on their chest. Their faces were covered. Even
if they were pretty far away, I could make up their features
. . . long almond-shaped eyes. Their faces were oval, but their
chins seemed to be square, and they had high foreheads.
Their hair was covered with a headband of the same material as the cape, adorned with a precious stone. I think their
eyes were dark. . . .

I didn't feel restless in front of these beings that belonged
to another world but were so similar to us. I wanted to talk
to them, but in what language? Spanish? Magyar? I hesi-
tated, and then I heard a voice resonating inside me, like an
inner voice, and I listened. . . .

"Stranger, your wit has let you overcome the tests. You are
the first one to have the privilege to come to us by our own
will . . . our civilization has always ruled over the sun and
your planet: Earth. . . . These indestructible books include
the history of all civilizations: those from above and below.
Our knowledge goes beyond these stone walls. We consider
you our brothers, not lesser or higher beings, only different.
. . . Many among you know the secret. They have been help-
ing you for centuries without your knowing. Go back to

where you came from. The road will open to you, it will be easier, and we will guide your steps from afar. Do not touch anything that does not belong to you; otherwise you will never again find the path that leads to your sun."

Andreas Faber-Kaiser, editor of the magazine *Mundo Desconocido* (Unknown world), tried to interview Guinchard and Paolantoni to confirm if what Moricz narrated was true, but they never confirmed the story.

In "La cruz del diablo" (The devil's cross), his only article about the Tayos Cave, Andreas tells his story and refers to that book: "In 1987 I tried to locate the authors. I wanted to get in touch with them because they had gotten information from Moricz fourteen years before. During the winter of 1991 I went many times to their home in Paris, but never got to talk to them face to face."

This was typical of these adventurers and explorers. Surely they altered their conversation with Moricz according to their own wishes. This is nothing new to fans of fantastic realism. It is also interesting to see that in this version Moricz is the only witness, which is very similar to Jaramillo's experiences, even though it was stated that Jaramillo had the company of guides and Jíbaros since the beginning of the story. Both cases are interesting because they both rely on narrations and individuals. A similar lack of witnesses and evidence surrounds the creation of the Book of Mormon, a story that, as we will see in the next chapter, also becomes entangled with the Tayos Caves.

6

The Mormon Expedition to the Tayos Cave (1968)

Although Moricz's 1969 expedition for the Ecuadorian Corporation of Tourism (CETURIS) was the most famous one of that decade, a year before, he and Julio Goyén Aguado had organized a previous expedition to one of the Tayos Caves. Two important Mormons had gotten in touch with him through some friends of Aguado. Fascinated with the story, the Mormons financed this expedition and accompanied Moricz on it.

For those who don't know the history of the Mormon religion, I will briefly explain its genesis. Around 1823, a young American named Joseph Smith was working as a contractor when a being surrounded by light appeared to him, saying he was a divine emissary called Moroni. He told Smith there was a place not far away where there was a book of golden plates under some stones, and it contained the history and origin of ancient American civilizations. With those golden pages there was a sort of breastplate to which you could attach two transparent crystals, bound by silver bows, forming what was called the Urim and Thummim, with which you could read the plates.

Smith said Moroni started quoting prophecies from the Old Testament, warning him that when he found the artifacts he shouldn't show them to anyone; if he did, he would put his life in danger. As this happened, Smith had a vision of the place where the objects were buried. Shortly afterward, Smith set off in search of the place, the hill Cumorah in northern New York State. There, Smith said,

> Under a large stone I found the plates in a box made of stone. The stone covering them was thick and curved in the middle, and thinner on the sides, so the central part protruded and the edges were buried in the earth. I discovered the stone, used a lever on a side and lifted the lid with great effort. When I looked inside I found the plates, the Urim, and the Thummim, as the character described. The box where I found them was made of stones glued together by some sort of mortar. On the bottom, there were two stones perpendicular to the box, and over those stones there were the plates and other objects.

But the golden plates are not the only similarity between the Tayos Caves and the story of the creation of the Book of Mormon. I have always been surprised by toponymical synchronicities, and here is another. The Tayos Caves are located in the province of Morona-Santiago, which sounds a lot like the name *Moroni*. At any rate, the similarity between Smith's story and Moricz's explains why Mormon scholars were interested in the metallic library. They accept the claim that the plates could reappear on other parts of the planet, because no others were found in North America, and it was believed that Moroni hid them someplace in the Andes, in the Amazon basin.

LOOKING FOR THE GOLD PLATES IN THE ECUADORIAN JUNGLE

Hoping to find golden plates similar to those retrieved by Joseph Smith, the Mormons requested Moricz's guidance. Their joint expedition happened before Moricz made his sworn statements, and it ended badly, because Moricz would not take the Mormons to the chamber of the metallic plates. He took them only to one of the smaller caves, which had a horizontal entrance and was connected to the system of the Tayos Caves, which were similar to those in the Coangos River.

In 1999, a few years before his death, Avril Jesperson, one of the Mormons who had been on this expedition, told me that Moricz didn't seem to know the geography. This confirmed Jesperson's first impression that Moricz had never been in that cave and had definitely not seen the golden library. Jesperson believed Moricz was a fraud and a pretender.

Through my years of friendship with Aguado, he never told me that the promoters of the 1968 expedition were leaders of the Church of Jesus Christ of Latter-day Saints. I found this out after considerable efforts in Utah, when I located Jesperson to interview him and recover the original recordings and photos of that expedition. I would be the first one to unveil and publish that secret.

Jesperson kindly shared his journal with me, along with several photographs of the expedition (see plate 8). It seems that he gave the original Super-8 recordings to Aguado.

Jesperson wrote in his journal:

We came to the conclusion that the first step was to file an official request for the rights to explore a specific area which was likely the location of the cave with the plates, we needed to file the request to the International Court and then travel and visit, taking pictures of the discovery.

Moricz and Aguado talked to Jesperson about how they could legally and physically protect the gold plates and artifacts that, according to Moricz, were in the caves "taken" by the Jíbaros. Moricz told Jesperson that the value of the discovery was inestimable, and that once its location was revealed, it would be hard to keep it safe, even if they gained the legal rights to access and control the caves. Once the story was officially exposed it wouldn't take long for gold seekers, thieves, or corrupt government officials to try all kinds of strategies to get their hands on the treasure.

Moricz, who was usually paranoid, was not very fond of Catholic priests, because he believed the greatest danger came not from the natives but from the priests. He believed that when these religious men wanted to eliminate someone who was in the way, all they had to do was turn the natives against him, and they would eliminate him easily.

It seems the Mormon group followed the Namangoza River, because it can be sailed after it joins with the Zamora River to become the Santiago River. Moricz had assured them they could take a motorboat from Méndez and sail downstream for about a day, but the logistics made Jesperson doubt his guides.

Jesperson writes:

From Méndez we had to walk three days by land (which would add up to seven days total). It was clear Moricz had never been to Méndez because he couldn't locate important places in this small town, and he didn't even know where Dexel's office or the airport was.

Jesperson hesitates, and repeats that it seemed this was the first trip Moricz took to the area. They finally flew to Yaupi, which back then was the farthest station in eastern Ecuador. They took rafts downstream to Monje, where a motorboat would take them to Teniente Ortiz. There they found one Sergeant Perez, who would later participate in the 1969 expedition because he was a Jíbaro who knew the area.

The explorers continued to the Umbaya mission, which was run by Salesians. They stopped in the house of Calixto Sangoshe and met Miguel Azapa, who was also a Shuar. Half an hour after they got on the canoe they arrived at the "first" Tayos Cave. Jesperson writes: "I asked Moricz the day before if this cave was the location of the metallic library, and he refused to answer me." But reading Aguado's journals we have a different version.

Going back to the journals and travel chronicles, Moricz and Aguado were received by the Jíbaro chiefs, the cacique Nayambi, and the witch Jukma and continued on muleback and then along the river in a canoe toward the entrance of the cave. Moricz and Aguado entered the treasure cave alone. Aguado wrote in his journal:

> We flew with Brother Avril [Jesperson] in a small plane toward Yaupi, in the furthest reaches of the southwest, with pretty bad weather and through impressive canyons covered by thick vegetation. It took us twenty minutes, and when we landed, the Jíbaros surrounded the plane. After a couple of nights in the Jíbaro territory, we continued the trip by raft on the Yaupi River, and a little after dawn we arrived at the first entrance of a Tayos Cave.

This was the cave they found with Jesperson. They stayed in the cave for two and a half hours, but Moricz didn't show them anything. It comes to my attention that the story in Aguado's journal—of which he gave me a copy in 1997—does not match with what we read in other versions, even those that were published in periodicals back then. Julio's journals give us yet another version, with curious variations: "We unloaded our equipment and prepared our cameras. Moricz said there were two entrances in this area." This tells us that this was not the same cave visited in the 1969 expedition to Coangos, because this one had only one entrance known by the local Jíbaros and those who have explored it. "The entrance we took was pretty tight, and he had to crouch down to get in. We got to a hall of about 81 feet high, 327 feet long and 48 wide. Large non-crystallized deposits of water hung from the ceiling. We tried to take photographs but the flashes didn't work, we tried again but they failed again, over and over again, until we stopped trying to take pictures and started exploring." This didn't happen when I went there in the early 2000s, but the humidity in the caves is intense, and we don't know if the cameras and batteries of that time had the same resistance they do now.

Aguado, Moricz, and a couple of Jíbaros continued through a narrow gallery that had openings on the sides. They walked for about one mile, moving away from the natural light of the entrance. The cave continued through an uneven pass that forced the explorers to crawl and stand at times. These are the shapes of the Tayos Caves, which were formed by continuous overlapped water streams and geological intrusions that are even older than the calcareous element.

We read in Aguado's journal: "Suddenly we heard a screech, a terrifying cry. 'Tayos!' said one of the natives. We illuminated the ceiling and saw ten or twelve birds protesting our intrusion. We kept on walking through the wet cave until we reached another clearing that had light from the outside; the Jíbaros caught three of those birds."

Tayos chicks are very coveted by the Shuar Indians. They go on long pilgrimages at different times of the year with the sole objective of collecting the oil that accumulates in the birds' legs and peritoneum, a product of their constant diet of resinous almonds and tropical laurel and of the chicks' lack of muscle movement. This is why they are also called oilbirds. Their feathers are gray, with small marks and black-and-white spots. They have small blue eyes, which can't stand a lot of sunlight.

Jesperson notes:

We discovered many animals inhabiting the caves: spiders, snakes, scorpions, and a couple of jaguar cubs that dwelled in the small galleries located close to the surface, looking at us with confused eyes. We also found pieces of ceramics, human skeleton remains, stone chairs, and carved walls and ceilings; we could even say these caves had a different composition than the other caves we had explored so far. I think they are natural formations, but at some point a group of human beings lived in them. In other words, these have a natural geology, but men lived in them and left their footprints.

We were in the Tayos Cave only for one day, from morning until the early evening. At the end we took some pictures, but they didn't come out. We were guests of the Jíbaros, and they would have considered it an insult if we tried to take things with us.

As for the caves, in the few miles we walked we didn't find any other entrances, but the air wasn't rarefied, and the Jíbaros swore there were other exits. As a sign of our friendship we gave them a series of articles like machetes, good knives, penknives, and clothes, things that would be truly useful for them, and then we went back to civilization.

THE SIGHTING OF THE METALLIC LIBRARY

Moricz always played the same game of refusing to take visitors to the cave if his demands were not met.

From what Aguado said in a couple of interviews in Ecuador and in Argentina, I have been able to reconstruct what he and Moricz experienced in that short period of time they were separated from Jesperson.

After walking for about an hour, Moricz and Aguado arrived at a chamber that had a table with seven chairs, all carved in stone. Then they followed a short tunnel and reached a hall with a vaulted ceiling and walls decorated with paintings and images. This hall connected to two other smaller halls, and to get to them you had to crawl through a narrow, bent passageway. In this central chamber they found a sort of semitranslucent sarcophagus. The lid of the box was made of quartz and had a bizarre body that emanated an inexplicable aura.

From my analysis and research, I concluded that Moricz must have been in that chamber before Aguado, approximately between 1965 and 1967. Moricz told him after this experience, which he described in his journal, that he would take full responsibility if they were accused of desecrating the place (something I would also fear and experience during my expeditions). So Moricz accepted his fate and the consequences of a curse that could fall upon those who dared trespass the sacred and millennia-old halls.

In a second chamber Moricz and Aguado found some skeletons that were smaller than those of the average person. The first body seemed to be covered in gold. After walking through a narrow edge, they entered a chamber that was 262.5 feet long. Here Moricz saw thousands of metal plates that, from their gray color, seemed to be made of nickel. They were placed against one of the walls where hundreds of those metal and copper plates were piled, and they contained hieroglyphs, and cuneiform and ideographic writings of different provenance.

The two men also saw statues made of gold and stone, which represented animals from the five continents, and human-shaped figures in different positions and attitudes. They saw perfectly conserved Roman-like carts (similar to those you can see rusted in the Father Crespi Museum in Cuenca).

FATHER CRESPI'S PLATES?

How is it possible that a collection of Salesians, revisionists, journalists, and profiteers conspired to make known the story of the plates, especially when these resurfaced after Moricz and Aguado's death? Are these plates really from the metallic library in the Tayos Cave? Or are these the plates of Father Crespi's collection? Sadly, I believe that the plates Moricz used belonged to Father Crespi, a Salesian who lived in the area in the twentieth century and was known to collect artifacts and art.

Not many plates have resurfaced after the death and testament of Aguado, and they all coincide with photographs of Father Crespi's plates, which Moricz had taken and sent to Buenos Aires. I saw and filmed these photos in Aguado's daughter's house, and their labels said they came from Cuenca in 1971. To verify this we had to go to Buenos Aires, to the Argentinian Center for Speleology (CAE), where Aguado used to work.

7

Julio Goyén Aguado

A Basque Mystery

Trying to elucidate the life and works of my friend Julio Goyén Aguado is almost impossible, especially because he is no longer with us. And nothing is more disturbing than being subjective about a person who always tried to be objective and scientific.

Aguado sometimes used masks to face his friends and those who tried to find him at the CAE, eager to know or dream about the subterranean world of adventure. "Those who come to our center don't know that deep down, we are more a spiritual or esoteric group than a group of scientific explorers," he said.

There was more to him than meets the eye. We affectionately called him "Basque" in our inner circles of initiates. One of the main initiation tests was to read *Erné,* an 1893 novel by Florencio de Basaldúa, which has long been out of print, and which sent us in useless searches through ancient libraries or used book joints in Buenos Aires's downtown. Finally, after years of waiting, a photocopy of the book came into my hands the same week I was trying to organize the expedition to the Tayos Caves. Aguado was eager to come, and he was also proud to know that an old friend would do justice to Moricz's story and legacy. But he would get angry when he was asked about the metallic library.

I had my doubts before and after the TV interview I did in 1997. But every time I go back to Aguado's testimony I get goose-bumps, especially when I wonder if it was all a fantasy, because there is a great chance Aguado told the truth, and nothing but the truth. I don't know if he was talking in signs, symbols, and hidden meanings, but I believed he was talking about an unequaled physical experience. I often felt that he could have also suffered from an obsessive mania, because I remember he would often go to the bathroom of his office on the first floor to wash his hands. He did it once when I was visiting, and he invited me to do it when he had just washed his hands a couple of minutes before.

Aguado always struggled with money, but he kept on inviting his friends to go to the cafés and restaurants along the Avenida de Mayo, which ran below his office. He liked to talk and be listened to. He had the gift of storytelling, and his affectionate personality would always shine in his stories, sometimes with a little humor or subtle irony mixed in, although he was never hurtful. He had some Basque in him, but there was also the inflexible personality of those from Buenos Aires who believe friendship is the first and last border.

When Aguado returned from the Mormon expedition of 1968, he tried to stay true to his deal with Moricz, in which they agreed not to talk any more about the facts related to the treasure. In a letter to the general manager of First City National Bank in Ecuador, now called Citibank, Aguado defended Moricz, saying that the Mormon expedition had failed because they hadn't really specified what was supposed to happen once the treasure had been sighted.

Around 1976, Moricz offered Aguado two of the plates (we'll never know if these were from the Crespi collection or from the caves), so he could show them to Neil Armstrong when he went through Ohio (the astronaut lived in that state). This was similar to what they planned to do to convince the Mormons before the expedition of 1968.

INTERVIEW WITH JULIO GOYÉN AGUADO

My doubts go back and forth, but again I hear that last interview with Aguado, and he seems so convincing. I first asked how he had learned about the cave. He was very serious and a little tense when he started answering my questions, but he cleared away many doubts that had been left unanswered for a long time.

AGUADO: Between 1963 and 1968, Moricz heard about the cave from tales and from the indigenous guides who took him to the Tayos Caves, or, better said, one of the Tayos Caves in eastern Ecuador.

He organized an expedition for February 1968 and had the support of a North American entity for general expenses. He prepared for it throughout 1967. This expedition included the presence of Mr. Moricz and a representative of the American organization that financed the expedition, as well as a group of Jíbaro guides.

Between 1968 and 1976 Mr. Moricz did several expeditions to the Tayos Caves. The expedition from 1969 became the most important one, because this was when he publicly and massively revealed the cave and what he found inside it.

In 1968, before this expedition, I witnessed the request Moricz filed with the government of Ecuador, which was finally legalized in 1969. He declared that he had discovered some caves and what he found inside of them. After the expedition of '69 he kept on giving declarations and shaking the European world in particular, so people from all parts of the world started trying to get in touch with Moricz. One of them was the engineer Stanley Hall, a Scottish officer in British intelligence. After the publication of *The Gold of the Gods*, Hall decided to travel to meet Moricz. Hall and Moricz then came to an agreement and planned the British-Ecuadorian expedition to the Tayos Caves in 1976.

After that expedition to the Tayos Caves, I participated as a special guest and met the astronaut Neil Armstrong [see plates 9 and 10].

The event was highly publicized, and it shook the world. I was invited by Stanley Hall, and I accepted, in a way representing Moricz.

Why were the recordings of this expedition never published? Why censor it, and why were many critics of an expedition that didn't find any of the claims followed by Hall looking to probe von Däniken and find some kind of treasure? In both Europe and Ecuador public opinion was condemnatory.

AGUADO: They filmed the flora and fauna, the subterranean lake, and an artificial tumulus in a specific part of the cave, where they found anthropomorphic disk-shaped ceramic pieces. But they didn't film what Moricz had declared he found in the caves, because they never reached those halls.

The only evidence we have is his request to the Ecuadorian government to be acknowledged as the discoverer of that library of golden plates and of the metal and stone zoo, with all the ancient and present-day animals that were inside that subterranean chamber Moricz claimed he found. So far that is the only evidence.

What were the contents of the Cuenca Library of Father Crespi and the Tayos Caves?

AGUADO: Moricz filed a public complaint and a lawsuit in Europe against von Däniken, stating he used the golden plates Father Crespi had in the basement of his church in Cuenca—which had been given to him by the natives—and lied, saying they came from the Tayos Caves. This created a comprehension problem, and afterwards every declaration Moricz made was considered a fable, like his official request to the Ecuadorian government.

This confusion von Däniken created affected the declarations Moricz made. So considering the harm, and since von Däniken's declarations were false, Moricz filed a lawsuit, went to trial, and finally won. Von Däniken had to make a public declaration to rectify his previous statements.

Can you describe the archaeology and architecture in the cave?

Aguado: There is an arch inside the cave the English baptized the "von Däniken Arch" when they did the topographic study of the first three miles of the "traditional" Tayos Cave in 1976. [To see photos from the expedition, see plates 11 and 12].

There is controversy among geologists, because some say it is a natural arch, but others say it seems to be man-made. There is a lateral gallery with walls and ceilings that seem to have carvings made by men, scientifically speaking. The Tayos Cave was an object of worship for a specific culture. I think that at some point these people could have worked on part of the natural rock, but I wouldn't dare speculate more than that.

The Tayos Cave that has been studied so far is a limestone cavern of natural origin that was possibly inhabited by an ancient culture that predated the cultures from the area, and they might have inhabited these caves for reasons I don't know, or they were used as a place of worship by the cultures in the area. The cavern's topography goes beyond those three miles. It does not end there, because those three miles are at the same level of one of the galleries, and it is very likely there are other levels underneath. We would just need to go down and explore those other levels. This cave is longer than three miles, and it is one of the many limestone caverns found in eastern Ecuador, bordering with Peru. There must be hundreds of caverns like the Tayos Cave.

A topographic study of three miles was made on the first chasm, which is about 164 feet deep. It includes the entrance, and goes down a vertical chasm, 164 feet exactly, and then a gallery opens up. Von Däniken's Arch is located about 327 feet from there. There is a lateral gallery that seemed to have crafted ceilings and walls, and a central gallery that I thought was completely natural; it is about three miles long.

Many expeditions took place in the fourteen years between 1976 and 1990. I participated in some of them with Moricz, but these were kept completely secret.

What can you tell us about the mysterious death of Moricz?

AGUADO: There are two opinions about this topic: he died of natural causes, from heart failure, or he was murdered. We were in Buenos Aires when we heard about his death twenty days later, and we were not informed when it happened. This raised some questions. He had a health problem the year before, but he had overcome it with a lot of difficulty. It wasn't absurd to believe he died of natural causes. But it was also possible to believe he had been murdered, because people had tried to kidnap him to get to the mining artifacts he had uncovered.

Moricz never owned or kept the golden plates. The library is in the same place, deep within one of the Tayos Caves, but in the area there are hundreds of caves, so it would be very hard for tomb raiders and treasure hunters, or any scientific endeavor, to try and find the place *without a guide who requests the permits and takes them there.*

But I can say that the library of golden plates exists, and Moricz had only been commanded to tell the world of its existence. *I repeat: Moricz told the truth. I was even on the brink of making a statement in the United States.*

What was Neil Armstrong's role in participating?

AGUADO: Hall's objective in inviting Armstrong was twofold: first, he was Scottish, and second, he could add value to this expedition that could be made known to the world through photographs or a book.

But Neil Armstrong saw nothing inside the Tayos Cave aside from the natural flora and fauna of the cave, or its natural structure. He didn't have access to anything, just as none of the members of that expedition had access to the library of golden plates. The expedition was a failure in that sense, because there was an agreement between the English and Moricz, who was going to guide the expedition but decided not to participate.

Is it true that the English tried to take over the treasure?

AGUADO: I was invited by the English, who thought that, once we were in the jungle, I could give them some clues that would guide them to the library. I have always been and will continue being a loyal friend to Moricz and the truth.

They brought Dr. Vagn Mejdahl, a specialist in fine metals, and I was his assistant in this expedition. They tried to find the library, but I assure you—just as I would swear to anyone in the world, just as I said on Canadian television*—without a guide or the corresponding permits, no one can get access to that place.

I don't know what happened, and I don't want to speculate. I will only say that when the pact with Moricz was broken, he knew he would not guide them to the place. Moricz had said he wasn't asking anything for himself, only that there should be international witnesses, and he started naming people from several countries who could tell the scientific world what he had discovered, or what had been told to him. Since this didn't happen, Moricz decided not to be the guide.

I don't know if the English or the Ecuadorians who participated

---

*To clarify, Aguado did not say this on Canadian television, but to Stan Grist (who is a Canadian citizen) and to Zoltan Czellar's son Joseph, who met with Aguado several months before me with the intent to access safes containing materials and information about the lost treasure of the caves.

Julio Goyén Aguado and Stanley Hall during the 1976 expedition

wanted to steal that library and take it to Europe or melt it down. It would be wrong of me to judge the moral behavior of those who participated in this expedition. But I have proof that the pact signed between Moricz, the British Embassy in Quito, and the engineer Stanley Hall was broken, so Moricz withdrew.

Who was Father Porras, and what was his involvement?

AGUADO: Father Porras was one of the scientists in the Ecuadorian delegation that went to the Tayos Cave. When the artificial tumulus appeared with some archaeological pieces inside the cave, Father Porras elbowed his way through the Scottish Rangers and the English scientists who found it. He said those pieces belonged to Ecuador. There was tension in the air, so I can't imagine what would have happened if, instead of some ceramic pieces, they had found the golden plates. There would have surely been a problem between the British soldiers and the Ecuadorians.

In the other expeditions you did with Moricz into the cave, did you see the plates? Did he show them to you?

AGUADO: I did expeditions with Moricz, as I said before, and they were strictly private.

How might the war between Ecuador and Peru and the Tayos Caves be connected?

AGUADO: One of the fundamental reasons behind this was the lack of delimitation of the border between those two countries. Since I know the area well, I think another reason would be the gold found in that region and the oil fields. Also, Moricz lived in Guayaquil, and he always believed the Tayos Cave was within Ecuador's boundaries. For the Ecuadorians, what might explain that last war was the fame of the Tayos Cave and the possibility that within it there could exist a library with golden plates. To me, that last hypothesis is the real one because the story of the content of those caves is the most incredible story I have heard in all my life, as well as the story of the Magyar origin of mankind.

[End of Interview]

Hall used to say that Moricz, like Jaramillo, must have had a "real perception" of the metal library in a particular state of consciousness or through an unusual experience that brought them to experience the library physically and realistically.

Jaramillo's testimony might also be true, because in the nineties he described things that coincided with Moricz's and Julio's descriptions after 1968. Von Däniken's exaggerated interpretations of Moricz's testimonies to illustrate that the photos really belonged to Father Crespi: "Oval-shaped table with chairs, with a lower part shaped like an N, and another part shaped like a U. Not made of wood or metal." Moricz also describes, as would Jaramillo and Aguado, the presence of a metal garden zoo, with about one thousand animals that included giraffes, elephants, monkeys, and spiders. It was an artificial zoo made of metal, crystal, and precious stones, a real treasure. He also described books and metal plates, all with engraved writings. He noticed they weighed about sixty-six pounds. There were other halls and other books with thousands of pages with writings that looked ancient and unknown.

8

The Gold of the Gods

In the summer of 1993 I traveled to Las Vegas to interview von Däniken about the truths and lies of *The Gold of the Gods,* his third best seller. The Imperial Palace Hotel was the setting of a new convention, but not of the usual kind. The members of the International Ancient Astronauts Society, founded by von Däniken with an American, Gene Phillips, filled the poker and roulette tables.

Someone introduced me to Peter Krassa, the secretary of the association, and he sent me to the floor where I could find von Däniken. I was really excited to meet the author of *Chariots of the Gods? Memories of the Future—Unsolved Mysteries of the Past,* a book and movie that greatly influenced my way of thinking and exploring. Later on I would discover the real father of the ancient astronaut theory was George Hunt Williamson, who was also related to the South American archaeological past.

The door opened, and a rosy-cheeked man who looked too tan and hot greeted me affably. It didn't take us long to start talking about the Tayos. "It's true," he said, "I never entered the cave. I lied. I did it because the way Moricz told the story wasn't the style people liked back then. Let's just say I embellished the story. I gave it a new layer of poetic white lies, narrated in the first person."

This testimony shook me. The rumor was true. But even if my image of von Däniken was shattering before me, I still respected the spirit of the man who revealed the "astronaut gods" and who had influenced my early incursions in the mysteries of the universe. But why did it happen this way?

There is a clear before and after in the story of the Tayos, an inflection point that happened about forty-five years ago, with the meeting between Moricz and von Däniken. At that point the discovery of that subterranean world was not really known—we could even claim it was a local discovery—but with the arrival of the Swiss author, the Tayos Cave became an international sensation.

The Gold of the Gods made von Däniken a star. This brought a wave of tourism to the area, especially explorers from North America, where the book sold millions of copies. Today it is easy to find editions from that decade in used bookstores.

Recently, von Däniken tried (poorly) to clear his ethical faults in a redundant and dismal book whose German title means "fake evidence," although in English and Spanish it was called *History Lies*. The title and the content of the book reflect the unclear statements of the author regarding the enigma of the Tayos. But let's see how this endless saga began.

Von Däniken arrived in Ecuador like a tiger blinded by his own greed, giving in to opportunism and speculations, inspired by what the news said about the discovery of the century. This is how von Däniken met Moricz and his lawyer, Peña Matheus, and they would take him to places that everyone knew were not the Tayos Caves. Moricz's modus operandi was becoming clear, and the people he saw realized he would not comply with the rules and codes of control regarding the Tayos Caves.

The scientific and archaeological community continued the controversy, which also kept the book in the best-seller lists in the midseventies. Von Däniken touched a sore spot, because anthropologists do not find it easy to accept that a cave in South America has remains of the oldest civilizations known to man.

Von Däniken tells us how his adventure began: "I met Juan Moricz on March 3, 1972. For two days his lawyer, Peña Matheus from Guayaquil, tried to reach him through telegrams and phone calls. I got comfortable in his office and had enough reading material to last me for days. I must confess I was a little nervous, because all the stories said Moricz was a hard man to reach. Finally a telegram reached him, and he called us on the phone. He had heard about my books! 'I will speak to you,' he said.

"The night of March 3 a man in his mid-forties [Moricz] stood before me with tan skin, heavy build, and gray hair. He was silent. This is the kind of man you need to talk to. My questions, which were impulsive and urgent, amused him. Little by little he started talking objectively and very concretely about his caves.

"'But that doesn't exist!' I said.

"'Sure they do,' interrupted Peña, 'I have seen them with my own eyes. Moricz took me to visit the caves.'"

But Moricz, in his famous interview with the German newsmagazine *Stern* would say he never took the writer to the Tayos Caves, nor did he show him the metallic library. Moricz's lawyer would vouch for him, as he did in the last years of visits and personal interviews (see his statement in appendix C of this book on page 218).

In an article I wrote, "When Moricz discovered the tunnel system, he was poor, and would continue to be so until the end of his days. So far he had discovered some sites with iron and silver, and he granted the exploitation permit to metallurgical workshops. This helped him attain a better economic situation that, with a frugal lifestyle, allowed him to dedicate his time exclusively to his explorations. Juan Moricz estimated that only an inspection of the tunnel system, without going into details, would cost about one million Swiss francs back then, for the installation of an electrical station, construction of storage spaces for devices, instruments and supplies, security measures, and even some subterranean work."

It is clear that Moricz was disappointed with the failed expeditions and the truncated contacts with institutions, which were often his own fault because he couldn't make up his mind about the topic. Von Däniken's statements confirm that the Hungarian did not lose hope about finding funding to help him clear up a discovery that had been keeping him up at night since 1965. But the real challenge was discovering if Moricz was telling the truth when he said he had never shown the entrance to von Däniken, and if the latter lied to his audience.

In *The Gold of the Gods* von Däniken wrote:

For all those who write to me and ask me to plan an expedition to the caves, and to give more details about the subterranean installations, I must specify: I was not a member of Moricz's Expedition of 1969, and I never went to the main entrance of any of the subterranean installations. Moricz only took me to a secondary entrance, and I spent a total of about 6 hours inside the tunnels.

As with all my previous books, *The Gold of the Gods* is not a scientific book. It is true the facts written there could be real, and they are. But I did decide to add a little suspense and humor to the bluntness of the facts, and I don't think the author should be punished for being creative; this is what writing is all about. Journalists may like it or not, but they do the same!

If we intended to criticize every case, there wouldn't be enough *Stern* magazines for it. Thanks to my editorial contacts I know the attacks against von Däniken are good for the business. And just to show you I am not as close-minded as my critics, I will tell you I don't mind, and I understand it a little. Even if sometimes it hurts me.

Moricz spoke the truth when he told journalists that I had not participated in the expedition of '69. What these partial falsehoods fail to mention is that I never said such a thing. But they shouldn't have said either that I never visited these places in the photos, because I did visit a lateral entrance in 1972 with Moricz. The photos we took that time were never published because Moricz refused to do so; he even threatened us, because he was afraid if we published them, thousands of frenzied treasure hunters would start showing up. I promised not to publish them, haven't done it so far, and don't intend to do it, no matter what you say. I am a man of my word. . . . In 1972 we came to an agreement on what could be published in *The Gold of the Gods* about this system of caves. It was clear I wouldn't disclose the geographic location of the entrances.

Years later, Moricz would confess to Stanley Hall: "von Däniken was not important to me at all. The truth is I feel sorry for him. He destroyed the greatest story of all time, something that surely broke him from the inside after his initial lie."

Von Däniken and his publisher were asking for $1 million from the earnings of the book, which had sold about ten million copies around the world, to be paid for a few pages, a small part of the book that Moricz invented, because he wanted to verify the content, the truth, something he didn't move a finger for. They had already offered him funding for an expedition.

"I answered Moricz's demands," said von Däniken, "and he confirmed to the newspapers the existence of the subterranean world and a metallic library. In the *De Bunte* magazine from Ecuador, in autumn 1976 (after Hall's expedition), there was a debate and all the participants were disappointed in me, because no treasure had been found in the Tayos Caves."

When *The Gold of the Gods* was published in 1974, the scandal began again. The book reviewers deformed the story, as did the filmmaker Ut Uterman, who would never finish his documentary on the Tayos in the seventies. Wilhelm Robertoff and Edwin Park were also involved in trying to tell the story.

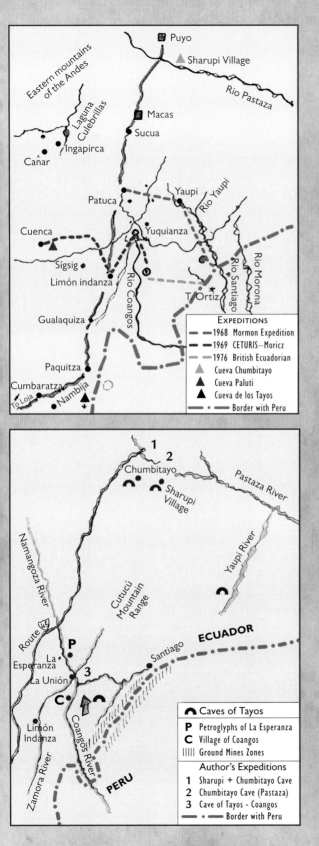

Plate 1. Map created by Alex Chionetti to show the expedition routes of 1968, 1969, and 1976

Plate 2. Map created by Alex Chionetti to show the locations of his expeditions.

Plate 3. Tayos hut in the fog of the Morona-Santiago province

Plate 4. Light streams into the opening of the Chumbitayo Cave

Plate 5. The author examining polished blocks
inside the Chumbitayo Cave

Plate 6. Gold on the ceiling of the cave

Plate 7. Fog near the Llanganates mountain range

Plate 8. Juan Moricz and Julio Goyén Aguado during
the Mormon expedition with Avril Jesperson on the far right

Plate 9. Neil Armstrong gets ready to
descend farther into the caves

Plate 10. Neil Armstrong (left) with Julio Goyén Aguado (right)
during the 1976 expedition

Plate 11. A picture inside the caves taken during the 1976 expedition

Plate 12. The Moricz Arch (formerly called von Däniken's Arch), the gateway or portal dividing the two parts of the main Coangos cave

Plate 13. Cluster of sawed slabs of rock (Coangos Cave)

Plate 14. Descending and exploring the caves on the Sharupis' land. Tayos caves system of the Pastaza River

Plate 15. The cascade (this image is from
the Sharupis' land in the Paztaza River region)

Plate 16. Alex escaping from flooding in the Sharupi Cave

Plate 17. Three officers from the Group of Intervention and Rescue who were part of my team

Plate 18. The cargo and generator prepared to cross the jungle by mule

Plate 19. The Coangos Valley from
Limón Indanza in Morona-Santiago province

Plate 20. Bridge over Coangos

Plate 21. Alex makes his way through
the narrow ducts and tunnels of the Coangos Cave

Plate 22. Alex inspecting the eroded walls

Plate 23. Interior of the Coangos Cave

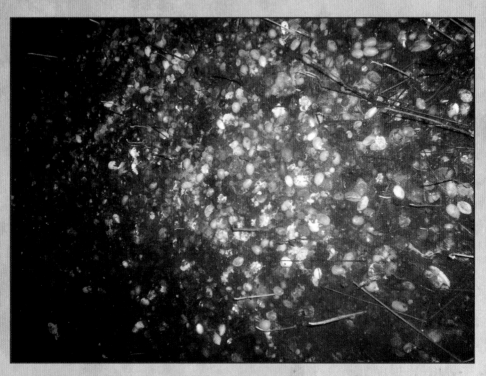

Plate 24. The ground floor of the cave, covered in Tayos eggs

Plate 25. Phosphorescent scenes inside the caves

Plate 26. Stone steps cut with laser precision

Plate 27. The cornerstone

Plate 28. The author before returning to the surface

Von Däniken's book and all the publicity around the world created the perception that Ecuador is a place of suspense.

Edwin Park explains the sensationalist version in a letter. Below is his testimony. The story von Däniken told was so fantastic no one would believe it.

> Moricz made a sworn declaration that is not based on true facts, it abused the Ecuadorian government and Dr. Peña; he made a huge drama telling the story of the lateral entrance we visited together. The scandal came with my book! It included the photographs Moricz gave me, and in it I described what we found in the tunnels.

Do you find this behavior to be new? I don't. Moricz was repeating his ambiguous conduct.

The document that von Däniken mentions does correspond to the protocol deed submitted by the explorer in 1969, which stated:

> We, the undersigned, members of the expedition to the caves discovered and claimed in Ecuador by Mr. Juan Moricz, formally agree not to give any declarations to journalists, radio, television or any other similar media, nor to publish any photographs. . . . Only the discoverer Mr. Juan Moricz, in exercise of his rights, will be able to release from the obligations and limitations established in the present document any of the undersigned when he deems it appropriate.

But thanks to Erich von Däniken's best seller *The Gold of the Gods,* the Ecuadorian mysteries came to life. Tunnels, gold, statues and statuettes, collections lost and found all came together to create an almost legendary image of a land of magic, wild loneliness, genius, and cruelty. Von Däniken wondered if the writing on the plates was writing from the dawn of humanity.

An article in *The Telegraph* spoke of plates with sound systems and incomprehensible drawings. At some point von Däniken thought of Enoch and also of the connection between this book and the Mormons. Zecharia Sitchin connected them with the Eter-Efi and Enki.

Von Däniken studied similar religions since 1959, when he began his planetary search for the astronaut gods. "Being in front of Moricz and his Tayos I learned to be amazed again, I had seen these crazy descriptions of Moricz in other cultures and geographies. I was amazed then," said the Swiss author, "and am amazed again when I remember those experiences. There are pretty old artifacts in some places of our planet."

Moricz, who never finished writing a book, said, "Maybe future expeditions will let us see this, maybe someone will write a revolutionary book about all this. The foundation of all religions may have come from South America. This book must come out at the same time in many countries." Von Däniken told him this was practically impossible.

"He also talked to me of a secondary entrance," von Däniken continued, "but I had to swear not to divulge its location. There was a river. Moricz got out of the car and looked around him. 'It's up there,' he said pointing to some rocks with vegetation. There was an entrance to a cavern, a black hole, and we sat down. Moricz had a square lamp. Peña Matheus took a picture of us there, the famous picture on the book cover. We crawled on all fours through the cave, where we could hear water running. I left my camera outside, with the priest and a child looking after it. We went into the cave, and I remember I saw some stone figures and some metallic plates I illuminated with my lantern. When we got to Guayaquil, I asked for the pictures from 1969 to use them in my new book."

Moricz and Peña Matheus forgot to mention that those photographs he gave to von Däniken were not his, but were taken by two members of that expedition, by Hernán Fernández Borrero and the photographer for the second expedition, who managed to take better pictures.

Although von Däniken made up his own expedition using the pictures he took of the artifacts in the Crespi museum, von Däniken's book was important because it showed the Father Crespi Museum to the public for the first time and brought Moricz's story back to life.

9

Father Crespi's Museum of the Impossible

The legend of the Tayos Plates is related to some of the metal plates (of copper, silver, or gold) that Father Carlo Crespi had gathered over the decades and stored in a classroom of the María Auxiliadora parish and high school in Cuenca.

The life and work of Father Crespi cannot be separated from the mystery of the Tayos. In 1972 von Däniken discovered these artifacts. Some have mistakenly implied that the priest was a cunning impostor who deceived his visitors. But it was the other way around: his parishoners and neighbors may have been the ones to deceive him.

Heather Leithman of MIT analyzed the gold collection in Father Crespi's museum and stated it was fake Inca gold, and that these were mostly gold- and silver-plated objects that only had layers of 0.5–2 milligrams.

It has been said that Crespi knew these plates were made of brass and not gold, but he didn't mind. He was trying to do more good than evil, and his supposed holiness converged with his advanced senility, especially during the last decade of his life. Moricz never stated that the plates were made of gold, but he did say they were yellow.

Von Däniken, beyond mocking the priest from the start, justified the errors in his book by saying, "Some treasures were found in

118

Juan Moricz's caves, which were moved and taken from the caves after my book [*The Gold of the Gods*] was published." There is no evidence of these claims.

Carlo Crespi became famous around the world, especially for Ecuadorians, thanks to von Däniken and *The Gold of the Gods*. Crespi's collection of metallic and stone artifacts eclipsed the life of an extraordinary character, a real Renaissance man, a pioneer of the arts and botanical sciences, a documentary filmmaker, and a missionary of the Roman Catholic Salesian order.

Sadly, Crespi died in 1982. One of my objectives was to meet him in order to shine some light on his connection with the Tayos, but the trip didn't happen because of another war between Ecuador and Peru that year. Crespi, like all our other characters, took more than one secret with him to his grave.

Unlike the elusive Salesians, the director of the Central Bank Museum, Carlos Abad, received us kindly and opened his doors and basements to us without demanding we bow to him. There we found a large ceramic and stone collection, as well as oil paintings and wooden art from the collections of Father Crespi, who is more famous abroad than in his own country.

The Salesian father Domingo Pérego told us: "Crespi was one of the first Salesians to explore the Coangos. . . . He knew the Tayos Caves and its dwellers. . . . But I don't think there is anything there, and I have been down there several times. The only thing we ever found was a tooth from an elephant, or a tooth from a saber-tooth tiger—what do I know?"

The director of the María Auxiliadora parish and high school, Father Alberto Enriquez, reluctantly told us that Crespi was being fooled by his own parishioners and neighbors, who copied classical images from art books and reproduced them in metal, ceramics, and other materials. Some of these were gold plates, and in the seventies it was believed these came from the Tayos Caves.

The Cañar and Azuay areas I have explored, hoping to find a key to the Tayos enigma, are filled with what I would call anachronistic and anomalous ceramics and artifacts. Some of them have inscriptions that are not from South America, but they aren't frauds from the Crespi collection. They are art crafted by the ordinary and parochial inhabitants in the Cuenca, Cañar, and Azuay regions. My interest in these pieces is how I got to the Culebrillas Lake, where I found evidence of a pre-Inca city that was dismantled like Tiwanaku, or the citadel I discovered in the Peruvian sierra I temporarily called "Zed," with granite blocks all over the place. Many of the constructions go toward the water, where more evidence will surely surface of this culture that lived where the two Inca roads (called Qhapaq Ñan) forked toward Ingapirca, the other (but smaller) Ecuadorian Machu Picchu.

Back in Cuenca, in order to continue discovering the truth, we insisted that the Salesians show us what was left of the unclassifiable Crespi collections. They were reluctant, but finally Father Roberto Guglielminetti led us to the María Auxiliadora basements.

It was sad to see that the order didn't take Crespi's collecting and museological hobbies seriously, because they had rusted tin, brass, stone, and ceramic artifacts of all sizes; metal canoes; brass solar statues; Persian-style military helmets; bizarre animals; and unusual flora and fauna, all stacked on top of each other.

It didn't take us long to offer Father Guglielminetti our services if they decided to bring back to life these disturbing items that the appraisers and analysts of the Cuenca Central Bank left untouched or didn't bother to classify. There are no traces of the gold plates that went to an exhibit in Austria: the Central Bank sent us to María Auxiliadora, and at the parish they sent us back to the bank. Where did the gold and copper plates, which were part of this extraordinary museum, end up? We all still wonder, and people still ask me when the topic comes up.

Another great mystery is the thousands of oil paintings from past centuries that Crespi had accumulated from European painters as well as from Cuzco and Quito. Few have been restored, and many need to be rescued from final deterioration.

Where did these paintings come from? There is something unexplainable in these collections, even if it was clear that Crespi was a devout collector for decades. Some say Crespi was a Nazi, and many of these works of art had been plundered during the height of the Third Reich in Europe. This was the theory of the North American researcher Colonel Wendelle Stevens, who found witnesses saying works of art arrived from Europe with Nazis who settled in Ecuador.

Crespi believed his collection included anatomical drawings made by Leonardo da Vinci, Raphael, and Cimabue, a Madonna by Botticelli, and a Tintoretto. It is believed he had forty or fifty works from the great masters of the Renaissance. Many of the founders of the Salesian order came from great Italian families, and many of these families had these paintings.

In the early seventies an Italian-American explorer, Pino Turolla, wrote about Juan Moricz, Petronio Jaramillo, and Father Crespi. In his book *Beyond the Andes,* he contended that many of the artifacts in Father Crespi's collection came from the Tayos Caves. He believed the natives paid him for ecclesiastical favors with golden plates and artifacts they knew would interest Crespi, who never refused to help those in need.

How could we determine if the plates came from the Tayos Caves? How could we prove forgers existed and went without punishment? We have tried to find some of the culprits, but no one has testified yet.

Crespi said that items came from the Ingapirca ruins, "from a culture that existed long before the Incas arrived. When my father died in Italy, he left me the mission of saving some ancient treasures from greedy hands and the black market."

In the late sixties and early seventies, Crespi told Pino Turolla that he was interested in the civilizations from Mesopotamia and Egypt, in the maritime expansion of the Phoenicians, and in the Inca and Mesoamerican cultures.

In Father Crespi's collection there were a dozen boxes. Each one had four to six golden metal plates, with a relief showing dragons, camels, elephants, palm trees, pyramids, half-moons, stars, and sun symbols. Crespi used to say: "These are my golden and silver treasures." There was a plate that represented the commandments of the Egyptian pharaohs. Father Crespi used to say to the natives, "If you find something like this, bring it to me, and I will reward you."

Turolla believed many of the plates came from the Chorrera culture, four thousand years old. The ancient Chorreras may have descended from the high plains, between the middle and eastern mountain ranges of the Andes, from places called Alausí, Cerro Narío, and Descanso. But what intrigued Turolla in the seventies were the sites discovered in the area of Loja, near the banks of the Zamora River, a river with direct access to the lowlands of the Amazon basin. The ceramics of the Chorrera culture have elements traditionally associated with the tropical Amazon forest.

For me, the answer lay more in the Azuay and Cañar zones than anywhere else. Many of the crafts of the Cañar area are similar to the style of the handcrafted metals and ceramics that were left out of the Central Bank's collection.

10

Past Stories, Recent Searches

During my first trip to Guayaquil in 2006, I interviewed Gastón Fernández Borrero, who organized the first official expedition to the Tayos Caves in 1969.

His faculties and memory were affected from a recent illness and an accident, but I can only say the man I met was a colorful person, who was also honest and direct. His main concern was that in that same year (2006), the English would reveal a secret document of the expedition of 1976, after the Public Records Act could be applied thirty years after the event.

Gastón, as people called him on the Ecuadorian coast, had recently published a work of notes and memos of the expedition of 1969 (*My Two Trips to the Tayos Caves* and *The Border Problem between Ecuador and Peru*).

What bothered Gastón was that, as he said, "the English left without leaving a final report of the expedition." This obsession would lead him to send letters to the British queen—which of course went unanswered—to highlight his theory that archaeological pieces and plates from the metallic library had been extracted during that expedition. We know that there was tension between the Ecuadorian archaeological division, led by Father Porras and

Hernán Crespo Toral, and the British scientists. With his own eyes Aguado witnessed the priest throwing himself over one of the loads, trying to prevent it from being taken up to the surface.

The archaeologist and TV producer Presley Norton, who would also participate in the 1976 expedition, said, "Ecuadorians found remains of civilizations that dated back to 1000–1500 BC." It seems Father Pedro Porras, who worked for the archaeology department of the Pontificia Universidad Católica del Ecuador (PUCE) carbon-dated the artifacts, and his results were more reliable than those of the British, who used the thermoluminescence system.

Norton told Gastón the British Empire always chose the best alumni from the universities of Cambridge and Oxford to send to the other side of the "Black Wall," meaning a training site in the Tibetan Himalayas, where they were trained as superspies, who then served in Scotland Yard and MI9. While there is not yet proof that Hall was part of British intelligence, it is the hypothesis of many involved in the Tayos mystery.

During the July 1969 expedition, Gastón asked Moricz why the affluent of the Santiago River was called the Coangos (or Kuankus), and he answered that *cuk* means *kitchen* in almost every language in the world, because in ancient times heated stones were used for cooking. *Cuk* means *stone* and *angus* means *angels*, so the name of the river meant *stone angels*. He also derived other Ecuadorian words from Magyar roots: Guayaquil, for example, came from *gus*, meaning *first; haya,* which means *mother;* and *quil*, which tranlates to *town*.

When asked about the metallic library and the 1969 expedition, Gastón told me, "The conversations with Moricz after we left Guayaquil for Limón Indanza were recurring and repetitive about his theory of the metallic library in the caves—written in Magyar—whose discovery and dissemination would cause a world revolt."

The 1969 expedition group left from Guayaquil to Cuenca by car and truck, then from Limón on muleback until they reached

El Pescado, Tres Copales, La Esperanza, and La Unión. They continued by canoe to La Puntilla, a peninsula on the Santiago River, near its connection to the Coangos River. They went on by foot to the Jíbaro land in Jukma, the domain of a Coangos witch, and they continued to the camp settlement in the part of the Jíbaro land that belonged to Guajaro or Guajare, a shaman.

In the cave, they descended 262 feet, and at the bottom they found an avenue 197 feet wide and about a third of a mile long, with 12 percent grade in relation to the ceiling or mountains at the surface. Moricz calculated that this thoroughfare was 500,000 years old. He stated that "there are other passageways and symmetrical halls that lead to other avenues; some are lower and others are higher than the central avenue; all are made with natural slab stone, crafted by men. There is no doubt these were used as refuge for ancient humans who have been forgotten with time."

Moricz was the first to be surprised by the weird stones and symmetrical blocks inside the caves. He wondered out loud, in front of the whole expedition, "Why were the stones cut and moved to the second gallery, stacked up like a loaf of bread, and cut in slices with evident use of precision devices?" (See plate 13, which shows slabs of cut rock.)

JARAMILLO ENTERS THE SCENE

Gastón Fernández Borrero's testimony brings me to the story of Jaramillo, as Borrero had once tried to invite Jaramillo on an expedition. Captain Petronio Jaramillo Abarca told his story to Patricia Aulestia, the archaeologist Costales, Andrés Fernández Salvador Zaldumbide (who told it to Borrero), and Moricz. Later, Jaramillo would also share his story with Stanley Hall.

Years ago in Ecuador they had a tradition of raising children from the mountains with the Jíbaro children. When Jaramillo gained the rank of second lieutenant, the graduates had to do at least one year of service in the east. One night he was dining in the Jíbaro land, close to the meeting of the Santiago and Coangos Rivers, when he noticed a Jíbaro staring intently at him. He suddenly recognized a childhood friend—a boy who had been raised with Jaramillo's family. Because of this friendly relationship, the Jíbaro offered to take him to a place he had only shown to his father. He mentioned he had promised not to show this place to anyone else; otherwise, he and his family would be punished.

Jaramillo promised he wouldn't tell the secret to anyone, and they organized a trip along the Santiago River. They even had to swim short distances to enter a small cave that had nothing special in it. But after they had walked a few feet, the cave started getting bigger. They kept on walking and found a large cave with giant metal animals such as giraffes and elephants. But the most important thing was not these animals, but the library, written in the Magyar language on metallic plates, although they never specified which kind of metal.

Gastón Fernández Borrero wrote in his book: "I should mention that when I did my first trip to the caves with Juan Moricz, who had never talked to me of Captain Petronio Jaramillo Abarca, and before my second trip with the military men, I coordinated, with my good friend Andrés Fernández Salvador Zaldumbide, an expedition to the caves with Captain Jaramillo, whom I located in the city of Esmeraldas. I visited him and invited him to a possible expedition, and he politely said he would not join us. This was the background I had. Some of this information I came across casually, and other information I researched before I knew anything about Juan Moricz, with whom I always maintained a cordial friendship."

Years before, Jaramillo had noted:

1. The cave had a steep entrance from the riverbed.
2. The access to the treasure chamber is through an underwater

passageway inside the cave, with a top that is visible during the dry season from October to March.

3. The treasure is located under the river.

The exact location is marked by hearing an increase in the murmur of the waterfall. He said the chamber could be found after a thirty-minute walk through the cave, and when thunder and lightning strike, the metallic library could be seen.

Jaramillo also described crystal boxes and golden skeletons. He could have been talking about two places: Loja, founded in 1536, or Zamora, which is 33.5 miles from Loja.

Years before, Hall had written, "The search should focus on the province of Pastaza, south of the community of Canelos—15.5 miles south of Puyo—in the territory that goes as far as the limits of the Pastaza River. There is a system of caves in the jaguar country, one day and a half walk southeast of Canelos, near the confluence of the Bombonoza and Umupi Rivers. The region is filled with caves where tayos birds live, but in a smaller amount than the Coangos caves." However, the main entrance is located on the banks of the Pastaza River, a two-hour walk downriver from the hanging bridge in the land of the Sharupi. (To see photos of me exploring these caves, see plates 14, 15, and 16.)

JARAMILLO'S STORY

Jaramillo's widow would tell us that she didn't believe her husband.

I knew it wasn't true. Jaramillo first told his story after he tried to find Mashutaka, who was also called Pinchupe or Shushubin, known as Daniel Vega. This man's father knew where to find the cave that allegedly had the treasures, but it isn't true he grew up as a child with the Jíbaro Mashutaka. My husband had an amazing imagination, and he was very talented, but his imagination was one of a kind.

He had many dreams; one of them was to take the Government Palace. Sometimes in our house there would be forty or fifty guests camping during the weekend; they would all come from Ecuador. At this time he was trying to organize a peaceful public force to lead a revolution. He had a way with words.

In the army he had a bad reputation. Since he had no discipline, they would send him to the wildest and furthest places, like the area of Limón Indanza in eastern Ecuador.

This is why we have to review the original testimony, which we have thanks to Pino Turolla, the Italian-American explorer who interviewed Jaramillo in the late seventies. Nearly twenty years later, Stanley Hall would also interview Jaramillo; but he wasn't like Turolla, who blindly believed every word because he believed this was his last chance to rescue a story that was vanishing after the 1976 expedition and that had barely survived Moricz's death.

Here is Jaramillo's story as told by Turolla:

Mashutaka and his father, the Jíbaro chief called Samakache, took me to a place called Piedras Blancas, White Stones. We got to the entrance of a small cave, and as we started going into the cave I noticed we were walking down perfectly symmetrical steps.

We arrived at a large vault, a basilica, carved with architectonic lines. The right side of the entrance had several torches against the wall which the natives had left on purpose. We lit one and kept on walking toward a circular platform that had openings leading to various levels. We walked straight to a canal that had water flowing three feet deep.

We stepped into the water, fording the canal, and got to the other side of the cave, to a vaulted chamber where a little sunlight penetrated somewhere through the ceiling and made the crystalline rocks shine. I suddenly realized this chamber was not made from natural stones. These stones had been crafted by men; there were white, green, and black stones, perfectly arranged in an architectonic design.

This vault was as wide as the others we had seen before, and it had the dimensions of one of the biggest cathedrals in Quito. Right in the center of the vault there was a curved couch large enough to fit twelve thin people, or seven larger ones.

In another multicolored hall I noticed the ground was filled with "little balls" Ecuadorians call *jorutos* or *pildas*. The Aurichi tribes used them as toys. Some were made of a yellow metal and others had strange writings on them, something like modern shorthand or handwriting.

Then Samakache threw a stone and a round slab turned. He then told me the revolving stone door would go back to its original position at dusk because it moved with the light or darkness. When we entered the new hall, we were surround by hundreds of stone animals, among which were elephants, mastodons, reptiles, like snakes, and also coyotes, jaguars, horses, and birds. They all measured about 11.8 inches tall.

The weirdest thing of all was what we found in the center of the hall: a crystal coffin with walls that were 1 inch thick. Inside it had a human skeleton coated in gold. It was 9.1 feet tall.

Jaramillo compared it to the height of the natives in the Achuyanos tribe, who were slaves of the Auchiri. They had white skin, yellow hair, and blue eyes. The descendants of this "golden skeleton" would be the Achuyanos.

They moved on to a third room where they found eight figures that were half human, half animal. Some had the upper half of a falcon and the lower half of a horse. There were also figures of men with wings instead of arms, elephant feet, pig snouts, and long web-footed legs.

In that same hall there was a cauldron made of a yellow metal; behind it was the figure of a man with the head of a monster with golden teeth. "I looked inside the cauldron and found twelve children figurines, thinking they had been cooked and devoured there," Jaramillo told Turolla.

After those visions, they decided to spend the night in the cave, where the light from the outside reflected on the crystal rocks. The following day they continued their exploration and examined the other hall, where an arch held fifteen cylindrical columns that were 65.4 feet high.

From there, they entered another hall that had shelves made of yellow metal, on which there were hundreds of huge books made of a golden metal with red covers. They were two feet square and six inches thick. The pages had symbols similar to those engraved on the little balls. Others were completely filled with geometrical figures. "They were geometry books," affirmed Jaramillo without a doubt.

The origin of the coastal cultures can be tracked to the Amazon basin. A large part of the eastern Andes is too high to take advantage of its trees, and these areas were uninhabited during the time these cultures developed until seven thousand years ago, and many of us think they could have taken refuge in the deep caves.

This would explain why, from the period between 18,000 and 9000 BCE, humanity could have transitioned from primitive hunter and gatherer groups to a highly superior and evolved culture, or at least a culture that was more sophisticated than the previous ones. This was a period of high volcanic activity and constant earthquakes, so the caves could have given refuge against earthquakes and landslides.

Temperatures got warmer twenty thousand years before our era, but the following ten thousand years had cyclical fluctuations from warm to cold temperatures, like those we have today, with or without global warming or the greenhouse effect. It is not so crazy to believe that cultures could have taken refuge in the depths of the Andes from the many catastrophic variations we had in the last fifty thousand years, especially during the last twelve thousand years.

Jaramillo told Andrés Fernández Salvador Zaldumbide he knew of a cave in eastern Ecuador that had megalithic shapes and excavations built by an ancient civilization. Many others, like Jaramillo, knew of Andrés's wealth, because he was an owner of one of the most famous mineral-water companies—Guitig Fine Water. Jaramillo also asked him if he could help with an expedition to return to what could be called "the Cave of Wonders." But Andrés was skeptical of Jaramillo's testimony, especially when he mentioned the oilbirds, because he knew there are many caves with these birds in eastern Ecuador and Latin America.

In 2008 and 2009 I tried to convince Andrés to come with me in an expedition where he suspected Jaramillo's cave was located. These new coordinates were not the same ones Hall had given us in 2005. Andrés believed Jaramillo's cave was located between Méndez and Limón Indanza, and he thought he could find it.

We talked for months while he continued his private expeditions to find the treasure of Atahualpa in the Llanganates, a priority that had consumed almost half a century of expeditions, deceptions, and hopes, as well as new incursions to the problematic zone of the Tayos.

When I returned to Guayaquil in the fall of 2009, Andrés was not as excited to go find Jaramillo's cave, especially not in his two-person plane, which he used to run away from the stress of the city with his beautiful wife to head to their coastal estate.

We had talked for over a year about organizing an expedition together in which we would fly over the area first and then continue by land once we knew the exact location, using his vast experience as a pilot and as an accomplished explorer.

As I said, Andrés believed the cave was between Méndez and Limón Indanza, an area that encompassed sixty-two miles and countless rivers that could take months or years to explore. But I soon realized he was hesitant, or he didn't have enough information about the cave system Jaramillo had found.

Aguado's papers contained notes explaining there are three doors to the Tayos Caves, and they are all supposed to be carved stones. The first door was near the meeting of the Pastaza and Morona Rivers, the second on the Tuna Chiguaza River, and the third one in the land of the Jíbaro chief Anguasba, in the Pastaza area. The entrances looked like a sort of door, and they all had a *tola** before them, which were used as burial sites in the Andes and other jungle regions.

Before closing, there is one more version of Jaramillo's story that should be considered: his own! What follows is Jaramillo's early experience prior to Moricz's claims.

THE TESTIMONY OF JARAMILLO TO TUROLLA

My cave may prove to be one of the more important discoveries ever made in South Ameica. I was taken there by a Jíbaro Indian chieftain, a great *cacique* named Samakache, and his son Mashutaka.

These two are very powerful Indians, and they are the only ones in the Amazon who know the location of this incredible cave. They were my guides. They led me throughout the caverns of the Cueva de los Tayos, and I tell you, it was an experience that has changed my whole life.

---

*From the Quichua *tola* or *tula,* a mound-shaped tomb, used by ancient natives.

The background of this story begins in 1941, when I was barely twelve years old. I lived with my uncle, a captain in the Ecuadorian army, in Loja, the capital of Loja province in the south of Ecuador. One day my uncle brought into our home a Jíbaro Indian boy about my age.

The boy was given by his father to my uncle to be educated. The little one's father was Samakache, who was a *cacique*—or chief—of a large number of clans of the Jíbaro tribe. This tribe lives in the South Oriente, and they are very savage, uncivilized Indians. The little boy's name was Mashutaka. Later he acquired the name of my Uncle Gilberto, so that he was called Gilberto Mashutaka. That is a custom among the Indians of this area: giving a godchild the name of the godparent.

Mashutaka and I established the very cordial and sincere friendship which comes naturally to the young and he once told me that in the eastern jungles of his homeland there was an enormous cave inhabited by big birds. That is just how he described them—big birds called tayos, with large eyes. He said it was a very deep, dark cave, and only a few of the most powerful leaders of his tribe knew where it was. That is all I can tell you about the start of my story in 1941. But the memories of this cave, this description, has stayed with me all my life.

Many years later, in 1956, I was an artillery lieutenant stationed in the Oriente. In that part of the country it was our practice to go out on routine patrols, and on one of these patrols I had a very strange experience—very dangerous and very impressive. My patrol and I were on the eastern side of the mountains, in the eastern jungles, and we woke one morning to find ourselves surrounded by fifty Jíbaros—fifty menacing men, threatening my soldiers and me.

I looked at the man who was leading this group, and I saw a face that had not changed a great deal. It had only grown older with time. It was Gilberto, my friend of former days. He recognized me, and it was this recognition that saved my whole group from being killed.

Gilberto explained that he would have to take us prisoners and lead us back to his compound to request permission from his father, Samakache, to spare our lives. This was something that could only be granted by the *cacique*. When we reached the compound, there was one more requirement. Gilberto demanded of me that I repeat his Indian name so that he could be fully convinced that I was really his boyhood friend. I can assure you that under other circumstances, to retrieve that Indian's name from my memory would have been very difficult. But standing before him and seeing his face, it came back automatically, and I could call out his name: Mashutaka. When we were released and left his compound, Mashutaka invited me to come back someday. I did so later, and that is where this story really begins.

After I returned to my garrison, I applied for permission to visit Samakache's tribal compound again. This was granted and shortly afterwards I made the necessary arrangements. With me I had the badge of army captain to present to the greatest *cacique,* Samakache. By tradition we, the military, bestow the insignia of rank of captain on the chiefs or *caciques* of high authority in the jungle. This enormously pleased Mashutaka. We spent the next few days discussing the customs, myths, and legends of his tribe—a tribe that in the past, Mashutaka believed, was descended from the fearsome nation known as the Auchiris.

Slowly I guided the conversation to that large cave he had told me about in his youth, with the big black birds.

After much discussion with his father, Mashutaka told me he would take me to see the cave.

Samakache, Mashutaka, and myself, on a two-day walk to reach this cave, far in the interior. No one else but my two guides knows the secret of the cave, and even today I cannot reveal its exact location. I will not do so until the proper time comes, when an organization will appear which, under God's protection, may support the full investigation of this secret, not only for the benefit of my own country but for all humanity. Until then, the location of this cave must be deeply guarded, in the depths of my innermost being.

As we walked, my guides told me more of this cave, and in my mind it became transformed from a rustic black hole into an immense underground cavern. They said that it had many entrances, some of them separated by a distance of a two-day or even three-, four-, or five-day hike. It was an immense cavern, with chambers fashioned by the hand of man, possibly in an epoch long before the Christian era.

From what they told me, I calculated that it must have been approximately sixty-four square miles in area. If we gathered together a hundred basilicas in the Roman Catholic world, even then you would not have an idea of the immensity of what I later saw.

This cave was just one of hundreds that honeycomb the eastern mountain range of Ecuador, where the Andes meet the lowlands of the Amazon basin. They are enormously large caverns, very deep, very long, with a great number of hillocks and peaks inside, a great number of levels, and many mysteries. All of this awes the spirit, much more so when one enters suddenly—as I did when, late in the second day, we reached our destination, and Samakache and Mashutaka led me into one of these caves.

For two days we had hiked and climbed for many kilometers into the interior. We crossed deep ravines and gorges, and then a plateau surrounded by high peaks known as Penas Blancas—white peaks.

Finally we climbed over the top of another small plateau and looked down and saw at our feet a good-sized stream. We jumped into it from a considerable height—something I had never done before in my life—and crossed it. Then we came to what looked like the entrance to a small cave. But as we entered it, leaving the water behind us, I realized I was treading on steps made in perfect symmetry. Now we found ourselves in a great vault, a basilica, hewn with architectural lines. On the right side of the entrance were several torches standing against the wall, left there previously by the Indians.

We each lit one and walked toward a large round platform, which in turn led to a great number of levels.

We walked ahead and came to a canal through which water was flowing at a depth of three to four feet. We lowered ourselves into the water, forded this canal, then moved up onto the other side of the cave.

We had been climbing steadily though a series of caves that apparently followed the crest of one of the ranges of the Andes. We came to a great vaulted chamber that was quite light, as the sun shone through many crystal rocks.

These were not natural rocks that formed this chamber. They had been worked and formed by hand—shiny rocks, white rocks, greenish rocks, some of them black—perfectly arranged as if the result of some architectural design. This vault was wider than any of the others we had seen, and had the dimensions of the largest of the cathedrals in the city of Quito. Right in the center of the vault was a large curved seat, big enough to accommodate twelve slender persons, or seven large or fat ones.

We continued along the left side of this vault, up some steps, and then found ourselves on a higher level until we finally came to a plateau, from which there were several different ranks of steps leading in different directions to other rooms. We followed one of these and came to the door of a large room.

Samakache and Mashutaka told me not to enter, but to look inside.

The room showed all the colors of the rainbow—yellow, white, pale pink, sky blue, red, and purple rock. On the floor were many *bolitas,* or balls, known in this country as *jorutos* or *pildas,* which the Auchiris say were a traditional toy of their ancestors. They were scattered on the floor, and clustered on the side of the room—some of them were of yellow metal, and others yellow-green. I looked closely and saw that all had inscriptions on them in a strange script, something like modern shorthand.

Then Samakache told me to step back to a safe place, and he threw a rock at the threshold of this room. As the rock hit, a great stone slab rolled down—a rush of black stone, which splintered Samakache's rock.

Samakache told me that this stone door would roll back to its raised position overnight. As they explained it, it used light and darkness to close and then open again. I have no other way to explain it.

We went back down the steps, then up to a second room. We walked in—there was no stone door in this room to fall on us—and there we found ourselves surrounded by a great number of carved stone animals. I touched them with my hands. There were representations of elephants, mastodons, reptiles, snakes, coyotes, jaguars, horses, birds. Some of these statues stood on small stands; others were placed on the floor. Nearly all were about thirty centimeters high. But there was one animal that impressed me exceptionally by the purity of its form. It was a brown cat standing on a triangular pedestal, and it had brilliant red eyes.

Strangest of all, lying in the center of this room was a large crystal coffin, its sides about 2.5 centimeters thick. Inside was a human skeleton fashioned in gold. It was quite large—2.8 meters long: I measured it with the spread of my hand. It was complete, with all the bones of the human skeleton, and each bone was fashioned of gold, as if to preserve the form of human beings who lived in another time.

The Achuyanos, a tribe living in the deep Amazon today, were often slaves of the Auchiris. The Achuyanos have white or fair skin, yellow hair, and blue eyes, and they are all more than 2.5 meters in height, very strong, and high-spirited. So I imagine that the Achuyanos are the descendants of the people who made this skeleton in the crystal coffin.

We went back to the central room, then took another flight of steps, even a greater number, to a third room. This room was something to terrorize any spirit. There were perhaps eighty figures—half human and half animal. Some had the upper half of a hawk and the lower half of a horse. There were figures of men who had wings instead of arms, or elephants' feet, pigs' hocks, or large fowls' feet. In a corner of this room was a large cauldron on a stand, both made of a yellow metal that must have been gold or very like gold. Behind it was the figure of a man with a head like a monster and gold teeth. His mouth was open, his hair hung down, his ears and feet were very large. He was sitting behind the cauldron, staring into it. I looked inside and saw in the spot some ten or twelve figures of children. I was deeply shocked, and my mind raced to those strange times when children may have been cooked and eaten.

We left this frightening room and went back to the central chamber. It was becoming dark. Night was falling, and the light that normally came in through cracks and openings in the rock, refracting and multiplying as it spread from one crystal rock to another, was fading. Here we spent the night and slept.

The next day we got up very early and spent all the morning, into the early afternoon, examining another hall. This hall was not made of pink, yellow, blue, and red rock as the others had been. This new chamber had an arch completely made of crystal of a very special color. The arch was supported by about fifteen cylindrical columns, between twenty and twenty-five meters high, some of which were reddish crystal, some yellow, some blue—but all similar in that they had at the center a core of completely white crystal, like the steel frame within a reinforced concrete structure.

We walked through this vaulted chamber, and my guides led me into a wide room, some twenty by twenty meters square. I looked around and felt fortunate indeed. The room was filled with shelves, as in a library. There were shelves on all the walls, and also standing in the middle. And all the shelves were made of yellow metal.

On these shelves were books of yellow metal with deep red backs. The books measured about two feet square and were about six inches thick. The pages were sheets of very, very thin greenish-yellow metal, with inscriptions impressed or engraved into the metal. On some of these sheets there was writing in the same strange script, resembling shorthand, that we saw on the small balls in the first room. There were also straight lines, broken lines, geometric figures, triangles, trapezoids, circles and half circles, tangent lines. In other words, they resembled books of geometry.

In all, there were about two hundred of these books. I took some down from the highest shelves, but could not put them back up again. They were very heavy—they seemed to weigh about fifty kilos—and it was quite impossible to heave them back into place. Samakache said it was quite all right to leave them on the floor. I wanted to uncouple one of the sheets, but my guides said that I could not possibly take anything with me. Everything was sacred.

They told me there were other such libraries, far away, and that it would take a long hike to reach them. This was impossible; my leave was coming to an end, and I had to get back to my garrison.

Our departure from the cave was as extraordinary, frightening, and dangerous as our arrival. We had to retrace our steps through all those strange chambers and again head for the canal in order to get out. I returned to the village, to my garrison, and this was the end of my experience in the Cueva de los Tayos.

But among all the hundreds of caves that exist in the area of the Tayos, this cave is a very special one. This cave I believe, is El Dorado. Francisco de Orellana, the great Spanish discoverer of the Amazon, heard this legend and left Quito with four hundred Indians in 1542, traveling east, to find it. He was unsuccessful, but he did discover the Amazon River and took this information back to Spain. Later he returned to the New World to look for El Dorado again. On his last expedition he vanished in the jungles of the Amazon.

We all have read about that endless legend, believing that

it is a city. Now I can say, yes, El Dorado is a city, but a city that is deeply buried.

And now I would like humbly to investigate the great ancient culture that inhabited this cave, in a scientific manner, without offending the interest of my country, and above all without offending those Jívaros I love and respect, especially Mashutaka, my boyhood friend, who will some-day be the tribal *cacique* of his clan.

The first son of Mashutaka was born when the night sky was tinted with red flashes, and the tribal legends said that this was to be the omen that he was to be named Yucalchiri—*yu*, or *god*, and *chiri*, meaning *son*. He is a kind of Son of God. When Yucalchiri grows up, not only will he be *cacique* of his tribe but he will also acquire the knowledge to decipher all those hieroglyphs, all those passages written in the strange script I have seen in the Cueva de los Tayos.

Mashutaka, following in the tradition of his own father, brought his son, Yucalchiri, to me to educate as Mashutaka himself had been educated by my uncle many years before. To pay for the education of his son, Mashutaka gave me a large golden piece shaped like a pear, and many other gold pieces through the years. I sold them, and with this money I was able not only to educate Yucalchiri but also to travel to many countries in South America to increase my knowl-edge. I know Peru, Chile, Argentina, Uruguay, Brazil, and Colombia.

In 1966, ten years after he brought his son to me, Mashutaka came out of the Oriente to my town, snatched Yucalchiri away from me, and took him without giving me any explanation.

I have kept the secret of the Cueva de los Tayos for many, many years on account on my boyhood friendship with

Mashutaka. Yet now he has taken his son away from me with no explanation, and he has threatened to kill me.

But I do not think the Jívaros are the sole proprietors of the great archaeological museum. They are only the guardians, because they do not know just what it means. I am very resentful that Mashutaka took his son away from me. I protected that boy morally and intellectually, and I received financial support from Mashutaka for us both. It was this support that allowed me to travel in many countries. Now I am unable to travel, and this secret, which belongs not only to Ecuador but to the world, remains unknown.

I have thought long and deep on this, and I believe there should be an organization of international scope which can provide the scientific support to achieve this discovery. The secret must be told.

I am determined to take serious people to the cave, although I understand that it will involve great and imminent danger for me. I am not afraid: this is a simply a fact. But we must go forward and overcome these difficulties.

Although he tried very hard for several years to bring researchers and explorers, such as Pino Turolla in the seventies and Stanley Hall in the nineties, the expedition of return and rediscovery never happened. Jaramillo was killed by one of his sons at his house, half a mile from the University of Esmeraldas, where he was teaching geopolitics during the last years of his life.

11

The War between Researchers of the Tayos

Our colleague Javier Stagnaro said, "When, after many years living in Ecuador, Moricz returned to Argentina in 1977 with the idea of finding financing for an expedition, he feared for his life because of all the information that had been revealed about his discoveries in the Tayos Caves, in the region of Morona Santiago, eastern Ecuador."

I had in my hands a letter written by Aguado proving that in 1967 he and Moricz had asked the then-president of Argentina, General Juan Carlos Onganía, for support to create a sociocultural entity to help with Moricz's research and to "enable him to finish an expedition to the mountain range of Ecuador."

We also analyzed documents written by Guillermo Aguirre, who wrote a unique but partial biography of Aguado and believed that in Buenos Aires they were planning to extract the treasure from the caves and take it to Argentina, from what I could make out from his letters. I have seen these letters personally, and there is no doubt that this topic should also be discussed, because it contradicts Moricz's claim that he had not moved the artifacts from the caves.

In the region of the Morona and Santiago Rivers, Juan Moricz had discovered networks of tunnels and caves that he said held "important objects of great cultural and historic value to mankind, like metal plates created by men that told the story of a lost civilization that mankind doesn't remember or know about. These artifacts were grouped in several different caves, and there are different kinds of artifacts in each one of them."

Moricz's idea was to build an on-site museum. This would have been hard to carry out and maintain through the years, and it certainly would have been looted with all the political changes in that region. He needed to find funds and logistical support from a neutral nation in order to have access to a satellite for his live announcement to the whole planet. So he considered making an agreement with an Arab country or getting money from the discovery of the gold and emerald deposits he had found during his explorations.

It is said Moricz became a licensee for almost ninety mining companies, so if his business was well managed, he could have come by an incalculable fortune. This fact, plus the information he knew about the caves, made him fear for his life. He was also afraid he would share important information with an inadequate media company, or that they would intercept and censor his announcement.

Andreas Faber-Kaiser explored the area of the caves but never went down. When he asked Moricz what would happen if he died before sending his message to the world, he said, "Nothing would happen. It would only mean I was not the chosen one to give the message."

An obituary of Moricz published in an Argentinian newspaper in 1991 said:

The Tayos Caves, a central point in the conflict between Peru and Ecuador, were discovered by the Hungarian-Argentinian explorer, a man with a brilliant personality, Juan Moricz.

On July 21, 1969 he gave a public statement where he said the caves were inhabited by the Belas people some 250,000 years ago.

The tayos are nightbirds the size of a falcon; they live in those caves and were sacred to ancient religions.

With his death, Juan Moricz took with him the secrets of the subterranean worlds he claimed to have discovered. The whole territory of the Andes has countless caves.

Moricz always tried to prove that ancient Magyar traditions believed that the astronaut gods came from the Ursa Major constellation because in Hungary, when an important person is going to be buried, they say the following funeral address: "From now on, the seven stars of Ursa Major shine brighter because our hero has returned to his ancestral home in the skies."

In Hungary and Ecuador, as well as in Scandinavian and Basque countries, Scotland, Ireland, and others, there are many tolas placed in groups of seven, like the seven main stars of the Ursa Major constellation. In reality, if we look at the tombs from the sky, we would find the image of the starry sky, which tells us these constellations are linked to the Earth.

ZOLTAN CZELLAR

In the last few years, Moricz's closest friends were another Hungarian, Zoltan Czellar, and an Argentinian named Felix Blasco, who lived Moricz's last chapter with him: the battles to explore and defend Cumbaratza.

Czellar fought against the Russian invasion of Hungary at the end of World War II. Years later he joined an expedition to Ecuador to find the treasure of Francis Drake. This is where he met Moricz; they shared their theories of human origins and of the search for evidence of giants in South America, like the remains of the giant that was twenty-two feet nine inches tall, found in Vilcabamba.

Czellar befriended a Father Vaca, who had originally met the family that had the remains of the giant in their vegetable garden. Czellar continued researching the giants—one had a head that was three feet long. Father Vaca showed Czellar some photographs, and Czellar wrote a letter to National Geographic, but they never wrote back. As with many of the enigmas of this area, the mysteries in this chapter remain just that: mysteries. Following Czellar's trail, in 2009 I would head southwest from Vilcabamba in search of a site where giants were alleged to be buried, but the address I had was fake, and it was obvious the people who gave me the address didn't want me to find the bones. I crossed spectacular valleys with my guide, who knew the region, and we roamed around for a whole day, following false references and dead ends, but later that night we got to the place where the rest of the "Giant" family researched by Father Vaca was supposed to be buried.*

Czellar shared his knowledge of giants with Moricz, and Moricz told Czellar he had found artifacts in the tunnels where he would take him, such as the metallic library and a table made of unknown materials. In 1997 Czellar died of a heart attack when he was driving a truck and fell into a ravine in the mining zone of Cumbaratza. Blasco wouldn't live much longer after him.

Among Czellar's belongings there was a key for a bank safety-deposit box in Argentina, which was supposed to have some of Moricz's objects in it. The Peña Matheus brothers came upon it, and they had different opinions. Carlos said there was nothing of importance in the box, because Moricz never left any trace behind, and especially not written documents. But Gerardo believed the key had to lead to something, and Joseph Czellar, Zoltan Czellar's son, agreed.

So at the end of the winter of 1996, Czellar's son arrived in

---

*Klaus Dona is a present-day researcher who has searched for and extracted bones that he claims are from giants in Ecuador.

Buenos Aires to meet Aguado, who was flying in from California. I remember he unsuccessfully tried to call me on the phone as I was interviewing Placido Domingo for the presentation of Aguado's grand book on the life of Constantino, which would come out later that year. Aguado brought the key that would open the safe-deposit box. Stan Grist and a TV team were with him; they were doing a documentary and a CD-ROM on the Tayos. In the box were some precious jewels, some archaeological pieces in the shape of lentils, more keys, old coins, and some copper sheets, the size of a bookmark, with inscriptions.

Aguado had held those metal plates in his hands during the first expedition to caves with Moricz, who asked him if he could take them to the United States to be studied. But later Aguado denied it all, first in a letter from 1969 addressed to Jesperson and later when I interviewed him in 1997, after Czellar visited him.

THE LAST PERIOD: CUMBARATZA

In September 1982, years after Stanley Hall and Juan Moricz had explored these caves for the first time, a psychic friend told Hall to urgently call Moricz and Peña Matheus. When he got Peña Matheus on the phone he told him, "Juan has found a mountain of gold."

He had rediscovered a seam or deposit in the ancient mines of Nambija and Yacuambi, one of the most important goldfields of the twentieth century. So Hall searched for possible investors among many firms in England, showing geological proof sent from Ecuador.

The foreign companies didn't take long to get to Guayaquil, but the documents show that Moricz rejected the business out of the blue when he discovered that the intermediary companies would not recognize Hall's commission. Mining companies came to take samples from the alluvial rocks in Cumbaratza.

When I studied the last five years of his life, it became clear to me that Moricz always refused to make money from his story; he believed it wasn't ethical. Aguado said, "He couldn't be bought and even less if you didn't comply with his demands to the letter."

The curse of the ghost of Atahualpa had alerted Moricz to the consequences of researching these topics. He had placed a cloak of protection around himself. The search for El Dorado, the wonderful land in South America, was done from the Llanganates to northern Peru. These were the areas he explored, focusing and remaining in the Tayos: his dream was so close, yet so far. He had a desire, or an obsession, to find a place where all the knowledge converges—an innate and primitive impulse to have access to lost knowledge.

In 1984, Hall visited Moricz, hoping to show him one of the books he had written on the topic. When Moricz eyed it, he grew flustered and accused Hall of using information from his personal library, as well as the knowledge he had shared, invading his intellectual property: in simple words, the typical claim of plagiarism we so often see in these cases. But Hall believes Moricz's anger was caused by the paragraphs in which Hall talks about the initial meeting between Andrés Fernández Salvador Zaldumbide and Petronio Jaramillo Abarca. Moricz always denied that he knew the story of the caves from Jaramillo instead of from his own explorations and clues he got through his contact with the Indios Colorados, natives of Ecuador, who supposedly gave some hints.

Moricz's "golden dream" had taken the corporeal form of subterranean archives and treasures that would dramatically change the way we interpret the human origins of mankind. How is it possible that there is a large metallic library in a continent where no developed writing has ever been discovered, aside from uncorroborated petroglyphs and ceramics of dubious origin?

Despite many years of research in the depths of the Ecuadorian jungles, the key characters in the mystery of the Tayos never succeeded in producing tangible evidence. Their narratives are tantalizing, but without physical evidence, what, or who, are we to believe? Though they created alliances to further the cause, the alliances were not without conflict, and each man had a reason to take his secrets to the grave. I had to keep searching to unearth the truth for myself.

12

From Scotland with Love

The Parallel Lives of Stanley Hall

S tanley Hall was born in Scotland. He fell in love with
Moricz's story as told by von Däniken in his book and then
fell in love with Ecuador. With him the opportunity to solve
the mystery was in the best hands, because he got to Ecuador
with the purpose of rescuing the mysteries of the Tayos Caves
for humanity.

But intrigue and distrust had turned Moricz into a very skeptical person, partly because he was very territorial, and because the
person who came to ask an audience and license to find the treasure
was a Scotsman who was a noble and an explorer, but who also represented an empire known for its scheming.

We don't know how Stanley Hall's destiny came to be as mysterious as Moricz's or Aguado's destiny. Hall insisted on continuing the search for the treasure, for the lost page of prehistory,
much in the way Moricz always said: "Either this is simple, or
impossible."

Hall began writing letters to Gerardo Peña Matheus, telling him
how he wanted to meet Moricz, but there is no doubt that when he
arrived in Ecuador in 1976 his objective was to do an expedition to
find the gold of the gods.

When he finally met Moricz, they talked for eighteen hours straight. This is when they realized they both believed Immanuel Velikovsky's theories of archaeological evidence for environmental catastrophes, which showed that Hall had a theory he had to confirm, and that, like the other protagonists of the story, he believed he had a duty to fulfill.

The conditions Moricz set for the English expedition were similar to those he had set for the Mormons:

1. the creation of a national board of notaries,
2. the presence of international witnesses who would testify to the findings,
3. that he was to be granted the leadership of the expedition, and
4. that none of the artifacts found could be touched or moved.

Here I also need to quote a memo from the Ministry of Defense dated July 29, 1976: "There is not only one 'Tayos Cave,' but several caves along our eastern territory in El Coca, next to the Palora River, in Yaupi, in Coangos, and in Zamora-Chinchipe, all of them east of the third range of the Andes. The day Ecuadorians learn the true history of their country and of America, they will see the great importance the 'center of the world' had in the past, and everything this continent gave to the civilizations on Earth."

Stanley—as his group of Ecuadorian and European friends called him—always believed that the fabulous illusion of the treasure of the Tayos could have been a tangible reality. He moved to Ecuador for it and later formed a family with someone who to this day defends and perpetuates his ideas. Remarkably, he managed to organize the largest speleological expedition of the twentieth century, and perhaps of history, in less than two years. Below is the official report of the 1976 expedition.

THE SCIENTIFIC REPORTS OF THE EXPEDITIONS OF 1976 (ECUADORIAN/BRITISH/SCOTTISH EXPLORATORY REPORTS)

Speleology

The Lost Tayos Cave system has everything for the speleologist: Waterfalls, huge tunnels and chambers: sporting feeder streamways and boulder falls of mountaineering proportions.

The cave system was a pleasure to explore, photograph and survey and ranks equal with the most famous of South American caves.

With the surveyed lengh of 4.9 km Los Tayos is one of the longest systems in South America.

The through trip from the "Cueva Commando" to Los Tayos is one of the most exciting and probably the deepest of its kind in South America, reaching a depth of 186 meters below the entrance of the cited Commando Cave.

The development of the system is classic in that the river which formed the cave has cut down through the sandstone to sink progressively further and further up its stream bed.

The original and oldest stream sink is the Archaelogical entrance which is in line with the main shaft and stream bed. The water now sinks in rubble over one km up the bed.

The "Commando" stream sinks just a few meters above the

entrance, and although a completely distinct stream, the two beds come so close to one another that it is difficult to believe that in the past, particularly in times of flood, the Los Tayos and Commando streams did not join.

In this way "Commando Cave" may be considered as a more recent upstream sink for the "Los Tayos" cave system.

We did not have time to confirm the hydrological links proposed on the survey.

The hydrology is complex, with streams splitting, sumping (filling the passage to the reef) and reappearing at frequent intervals. However, there appear to be three main streams entering the cave system. One, the Los Tayos stress, we must assume enters the system in the M6 inlet series.

The Commando water enters "Snovel pot" and promptly sumps. We propose that this stream also enters the M6 series, near the Cascades. However, it may also account for other inlets in that area of the cave.

The third stream, which we think now (having drawn up the survey) to be completely distinct from the Commando and Los Tayos sinks, enters the "After Dinner series" at an impressive 30 m waterfall which we did not manage to bypass. This proposal is of necessity tentative.

The geological controls on the development of the "Los Tayos" system, are striking. Possibly the most obvious of these, on entering the cave, is the variation in thickness of rock strata from the entrance to the lower parts of the cave.

Generally near the surface the limestone is massively bedded, with only thin layers of shale between beds.

The passages trend down, dip along a series of roughly parallel major joints, and pass out into unstable rock. In many of the lower passages there appears to be more shale than limestone and what there is of the latter is very muddy. The beds are thin and the passages show evidence of considerable collapse.

However, the situation is not simple, the dip and strike change considerably throughout the cave systems so that passages at similar levels below the surface are in different strata.

The rock is folded and possibly faulted, one case in mind being along the M6 series which appears to run along a fault with small vertical displacement.

Throughout the cave system collapse is evident in passage size dependent on whether or not collapse is present. The cascade inlet passages change from narrow vadose canyon type to large box section passages within a few meters, as a result of collapse. In the large entrance tunnels of Cueva de los Tayos passages are often of square section due to collapse.

As collapse proceeds the roof enters thicker and thicker beds and large gently dipping flat roofs result.

Because of extensive collapse there are few calcite formations in the cave and little evidence of flow markings from the streams which formed the cave.

Most of the passages are of vadose canyon type, although occasionally phreatic half tubes are present in the roof. Phreatic conditions probably indicated development before the gorge of the Rio Coangos cut down to its present level. However, since that time vadose development (passage enlargement by fast-flowing streams) has been the principal force in passage formation.

A number of features are of particular note within the system. The central Tayos chamber is of massive proportions due to collapse, and the roof goes up through the strata. However, at the upper end of the hall in the higher more massive limestone beds is an impressive phreatic feature, the Dome. This is a round, blind hole in the roof similar to the North American dome pits.

A massive reminder of the cave's phreatic origin. "Shovel Pot" gives an excellent example of the effects of collapse. The entrance passages are low and epi-phreatic, but a bedding plane leads suddenly to a massive collapse chamber, developed a major joint and quite out of character with the other passages. The Staircase and Amphitheatre cut down steeply through the beds and show the gradation in bed thickness very clearly.

The small active passages leading to the sump are steep and sporting, yet connected closely with huge dry collapse tunnels. These small passages may well be stable despite the presence of the soft shale strata, and they lead to the sump pool, which is perched well above river level due to collapse and the in wash of debris.

There is a little chance of bypassing the sump, but there are passages within the system which with effort would yield further extensions. The two of particular note are a narrow rift and pitch in "Shovel Pot" and an artificial climb in the "After Dinner" series, to bypass the waterfall.

Both require special equipment and are well beyond the regions explored by the Indians, in search of the oilbirds. It is however to the credit of the Aboriginals that they explored well into the cave.

The vine ladder on the 50 m entrance shaft impressed fearlessness upon us and some of their tree trunk traverses were positively frightening.

Here we have only covered the processes of cave development and the physical nature of the system.

These brief notes are only a small part of the fascination of this impressive cave and all of us were equally intrigued by the rich life of the cave.

The biology of the system is part of the whole cave story, the study of which is of undying interest of us all.

Radiocarbon Dating
Radiocarbon has for more than 20 years been the major analytical tool available to archaeologists, providing ages for organic matter recovered from excavation, for example: bone, charcoal, peat and shell.

The accuracy of a single radiocarbon date depends on several factors, including sample size, and under optimum conditions plus or minus 60 years is a reasonable uncertainty.

My role in the "Tayos Expeditions" was to assist the archae-ologists and to collect samples for C 14 analysis in the Nuclear Geochemistry research laboratory at the University of Glasgow.

A supplementary project was to collect speleothem samples from the caves. Stalactites and stalagmites can be dated by the Uranium-Thorium method, and oxygen isotope analysis can give information on paleotemperatures.

Speleothmem analysis is hopefully to be carried out by Dr. A. E. Fallick, Mcmaster University, Hamilton, Canada.

The excavations at the Tayos cave site did not provide any datable materials, however a "peat" sample taken from a depth of a 2 m may possibly yield an estimate of the rate of accumulation of guano.

Two sites of archaeological interest were located at the Mission of Santiago, approximately one mile east of the Teniente Ortiz base. The first site was at the site of the mis-sion, and pottery and charcoal samples were collected. It is hoped that the pottery will be reconstructed to its original form. An intuitive estimate of the age of the site was from 500 to 1000 years before the present (B.P).

The second site appeared to be considerably clearer than the first, perhaps about 3000 years B.P, the estimate being based on the decoration on the pottery, which was similar to the recovered samples at the coastal sites.

Charcoal samples were collected from the controlled stratigraphic section, and hopefully the dates will establish a chronology of the area.

One interesting feature of the archaeometry will be direct comparison between age estimates obtained by C-14 analysis and thermoluminescence methods used by Dr. Nejdahl and the National Museum of Antiquities from Scotland, Edinburgh.

JOHN CAMPBELL

Studies on the Oilbirds (Los Pajaros Tayos)– Steatornis caripensis

Reports from the local Indians stated that they normally harvest young oilbirds from the Tayos caves's system during the month of April.

In 1976—500 birds were reported taken from the caves. From work elsewhere on the species on average a little over 2 young are reared per pair.

This indicates that approximately 1,100 adults have reared 500 young taken this year. As many nesting ledges are too high for the Indians to exploit, there are probably in the region of 1500 to 2000 adult oilbirds breeding in the caves.

The very large deposits of seeds in the caves which have been regurgitated by the oilbirds after digesting off the pericarp (the nutritious part of the fruit) confirms that there is a large breeding population.

During the period the expedition was at the Tayos caves (6 July to August 3) the breeding season of the oilbirds was apparently coming to abrupt and with a number of young oilbirds failing to fledge and falling from their nests in a half-starving state weighing only one third of the expected weight, judging from the other stages of development.

Only a small percentage of the breeding population remained in the cave. 156 adults were counted leaving the cave for their nightly foraging on 14 of July, with approximately 10 to 15 remaining in the caves to tender and younger age.

This number dropped in a single family of young and their parents still present on 24 july, my last visit inside the cave. A final count of adults leaving on this evening of August 2 produced only 13 birds. While it is possible that the low numbers were partly due to disturbance at the cave the fact that the Yaupi caves were empty of oilbirds when first visited by members of the expedition on 24 of July suggests that it may be normal for the oilbirds of the area to desert their breeding caves at the end of the breeding season. This may be due to the large number of alternate caves in the area. In this behavior they differ from the species in Trinidad and Venezuela where breeding adults inhabit their nest sites throughout the year.

Large samples, from different points in the cave, of the seeds regurgitated by the oilbirds showed that the following proportions of fruit were normally being taken from the trees of the surrounding forests:

48% Palm fruits, Palmaceae
45% Mountain incense, Dacryodes species, Burseraceae.
7% Laurels, Lauraceae, and another unidentified discotyledon.

Three samples totaling 432 seeds, regurgitated during the period of the expedition, showed rather different proportions:

92% Palm fruits
8% Dacryodes
Less than 0.5% Laurels

Nearly all the Palm fruits taken were a species of Euterpe with seeds no bigger than 10 × 10 mm, and not extremely small compared to the bigger palms eaten much as Jessemia with a seed size of 38 × 23 mm. This is an indication of a very low fruit supply during the period of investigation probably causing the oilbirds to move elsewhere.

BARBARA L. SNOW

THE SEARCH FOR
A LOST PAGE OF PREHISTORY

The question is: why would Hall and others continue to search the caves? Why go through all the trouble? Despite all the nonsense and hypocrisy surrounding this topic, it was clear to me that the purpose of the expeditions of 1969 and of 1976 was to find and take over the treasure, or at least to have the opportunity to see and photograph it. In this regard, both expeditions were complete fiascos, as Aguado confessed in a filmed interview in 1997.

In 1998 Hall was going to do a second part of his expedition, but this time taking Jaramillo to the place; he would have English funding once again. He also told me he had earned the right to the location of the metallic library, since he had spent seven years talking and building a friendship with Jaramillo. "I think I know the exact place where it is located. The future will tell if my calculations were right or not. I think people can't critique my work if they haven't studied my writing first," Hall said.

I had studied him, I had even translated his web page and his description of the system he created called the Grailscope. I was very excited when I saw this name, because I thought it was an advanced detection device, but it was a system that synthesized logic with intuition using a database. He defined it as an interdisciplinary study of data from the Tayos Cave in relation to different disciplines such as geology, mythology, legends, religions, mysticism, philosophy, astronomy, and engineering.

I noticed Hall was a very polite person, and he didn't dare contradict Jaramillo. I assume something similar happened with Moricz, although he was more inaccessible and elusive when the moment of truth arrived, which is why Moricz's lawyer never dared ask him for material evidence of his discovery.

Hall also made some sense of the chaotic story of Jaramillo and told me what the original treasure would have included—or includes: "A library with thousands of metallic books, displayed on shelves that weigh approximately 44 pounds each. Each page would have ideograms, geometric designs and inscriptions on one side. There would be a second library with smaller, harder plates, but these are translucent, with carved parallel lines. Another hall would have statues of animals and zoomorphic figures in different positions. Metal bars with different shapes, next to a group of games and alluvial gold. An instrument to make buttons and simple jewelry. A sealed door, covered in semiprecious stones. In another one, a sarcophagus made of some translucent material [similar to quartz, but more transparent] that had the skeleton of a man covered in a thin layer of gold."

When I asked why the existence of the library of golden plates was so important, he answered: "Not only do I believe with all my heart it exists, but beyond being a unique treasure, I believe it is a chapter of the history of South America, and a lost page of the book of prehistory."

Until Hall's death in September 2008, we had countless talks, and I interviewed him many times for international journals.

HALL'S CATASTROPHE THEORIES

In regard to the advanced constructions in the caves, Hall thought most of them were natural formations, and that some may have been improved by the Shuar. The official report of the 1976 expedition said:

> The Tayos Caves are millennia-old mineral natural formations that have not been modified by men. They are a group of interconnected caverns or galleries that have different heights and widths, and a planimetric disposition that can be seen in the maps created by the technicians of the expedition.

In this report, and in several phone conversations, Hall insisted for several years that the formations were more natural than artificial. In a video interview from 2007—after my expeditions and testimonies—he held a more open position, where he was willing to consider the possibility that some artificial works could exist there.

In spite of his skepticism coupled with the open verdict of the geologists of the 1976 expedition, Hall had always been interested in the planetary catastrophe linked to Atlantis and the Andes. He liked the term *Antis* for the ancient population of the Andes; in other words, the Andean civilization that could have been destroyed by natural catastrophes. "The Andes today are very young in the geological chronology of the Earth," he told me in 2005.

Hall thought the mythical story of the creation of mankind

would include many keys to prehistory. One of his influences was Immanuel Velikovsky, the author of the classic book *Worlds in Collision,* who was one of the first people to talk about archaeological evidence of vast catastrophes. I was acquainted with Velikovsky's daughter, who lived in Princeton, so I offered Hall an introduction, but I was surprised to see he wasn't interested, even though at the time he was visiting the university for other reasons.

Stanley Hall was very similar to Velikovsky, but when the latter was mentioned, Hall never wanted to admit that he considered the father of planetary catastrophism to be wrong in *Worlds in Collision.* Even so, he followed that wave of mythic history and the relations between the solar system and humanity.

In the last years of his intellectual life, Hall catalogued and analyzed the history of interplanetary cataclysms, which happened when the planets were closer to Earth. These changes in orbits and planetary collisions with comets and asteroids, which caused cataclysms on our planet, were transformed by astrologer/priests into gods, goddesses, and angels, which would later be immortalized in words and stone. This is why many rulers are known as sons or daughters of the Sun, including rulers from the Egyptian and Incan civilizations.

For Hall, cosmology is mythology in action, and vice versa. As an engineer, he found similarities between the physical or geological world and the universe of legends, mainly creationism.

The Sun would erupt from other suns, or from a Great Star, leaving a trail of cosmic dust on the skies, which ancient civilizations would call Apsu Nun. Then the Sun ejected a great sphere of gas that would become proto-Gaia, which today is our Earth. The proto-Earth—or Gaia—gave birth to Ur-Atum, a creation myth that the Egyptians would develop over thousands of years. Hall believed Ur-Atum, proto-Uranus, was born from Gaia, the Earth goddess.

This might also explain how, for example, the mythical Titans, Cyclops, and Giants are large gas moons. The moons of Uranus—known as the Emperor of the Skies who was dethroned or defeated by the moons of Titan (pre-Saturn)—are captured in an orbit around proto-Saturn. The mythical Golden Age of Saturn came to an end when proto-Saturn was vanquished by his own descendant, Jupiter, whose serpentine tail would give rise to the myths of Typhon, Tiamat, and Ahriman. When Saturn created Jupiter, he also produced Neptune, Mercury, Mars, the moon, and comets.

Stories from the Arcadians, pre-Selenites, or Pirgios from the Mediterranean mention a period when the Earth had no moon, and when the messenger of the gods, Mercury (Hermes-Thoth), put the Earth in danger. Neptune, Saturn, and Uranus were cast farther out into the solar system as the netherworlds or Taieous, which Hall believed sounded a lot like the word "tayo."

All the great mythologies of the world tell the same story with different names for the same planets. Today, the days of the week have the names of the seven solar globes, which is evidence of the evolution of those catastrophic impacts that happened before the solar system became stable.

A SUBSTITUTE GORDIAN KNOT

When Moricz died, Hall was left like a disoriented orphan who would not give up until he again found a line of history that he could hold on to in order to continue his restless search. This line would be as frustrating as the previous ones. Its name was Petronio Jaramillo Abarca.

Hall worked on this friendship because he wanted to be convinced that Jaramillo was telling the truth, and this truth could be in a different cave from the one Moricz had been showing to people since 1968. It was like cutting through a Gordian knot only to have to tie it up again.

The hardest question for the Scotsman—which had consumed all of the protagonists, including me—was if Moricz had deceived us all, even himself, by stating the real location (and paradigm) of the "Tayos Cave" was in one of the many caves nearby.

Those who believe in the "conspiracy" of the Tayos still believe that Hall was a member of international Freemasonry, and there is a rumor that his special guest for the expedition of 1976, Neil Armstrong, was also a Freemason. Hall and his official biographers always denied that the ex-astronaut was a declared or recognized Mason, but there is evidence that Armstrong was affiliated with the Mormon church.

The rumors usually cross over, settling on the contradiction of the presence of an American astronaut hero in a speleological expedition to search for a treasure that could be real or fantasy. This question has caused rivers of ink to flow and has created controversies all around. Armstrong refused several times to give me an

The president of Ecuador (left), Neil Armstrong (center),
and Julio Goyén Aguado (right), checking a map of the region

Neil Armstrong poses with a stalagmite in the cave

interview that could have cleared up this recurring enigma forever. He always asked about my background and educational information. His official biographer couldn't help me either. The weirdest part, and the biggest coincidence, was that the topic of the man on the moon was connected to the topic of the metaphysical conditions of Moricz.

During the 1969 expedition—which coincided with the first moon landing—two events mysteriously intertwined in space-time. And who would have thought the first man to leave his footprints on our satellite would be—just seven years later—part of the first international expedition of the Tayos?

Another unexplainable thing was what Moricz's guide, Luis Nivelo, remembered. They were camping one night in front of the cave, under a huge full moon on July 17, 1969, when a strange shadow passed in front of the moon, to which Moricz reacted and predicted that one of the participants of the Apollo 11 mission would be a part of the upcoming Tayos expeditions.

Hall moved on, maybe hiding his apparent failure and recurring nostalgia in other projects that would justify so many years of expectations and illusions. As resigned as the Peña Matheus brothers, Hall continued thinking of the metallic library of the Tayos as the cornerstone of his life, always searching for a legend almost like the Holy Grail. He perpetuated it to exasperation and even boredom for himself and all those around him.

My research of the Marcahuasi Ruins led me to be interested in the Tayos, and my interest in the Tayos led me to Stanley Hall. This is how I became a part of that lineage of idealists and believers who would try to find an answer to the mystery of the Tayos. It didn't take me long to go back to what I had left on hold in the early eighties, and then in the nineties, and organize a flash expedition that coincided with the twenty-year anniversary of the 1976 expedition. So in 1996 I went back to what I had first attempted in 1981–82: finding the Tayos Cave in Coangos.

MARCAHUASI: PLATEAU OF THE GODS

In the hour-long conversations we had before I headed to Coangos, Hall said he believed that, even if his superexpedition had been as methodical as possible, they could have studied the von Däniken Arch area more. He also told me I shouldn't forget to take a good geologist with me to the expedition. I tried to invite Robert Schoch, who dated the Sphinx, and whom I had tried to take with me to the Marcahuasi Ruins, but the timing wasn't right. For Moricz, the expedition of 1976 "tended to take over the clues of the Supreme Knowledge, maybe to destroy all evidence or hide it forever." Perhaps this accounts for why it has been so difficult to pin down the exact location of the cave.

In spite of the first failed expedition to the Coangos region, Hall would alter the course of this structure to explore the area around the Pastaza River, which coincided with his new ideas. According to Hall, thanks to his Grailscope, he had found the location of Jaramillo's stories, something that I would personally—and unfortunately—discover after two consecutive expeditions to the place.

The tenacity and drive to find the truth had already taken hold of me. They had been inside me for twenty-five years, when my expeditions to the Marcahuasi Ruins had driven me to look for archaeological and anthropological evidence to connect with the Tayos.

Marcahuasi is a plateau in the heights of the central Peruvian range, almost 13,404 feet above sea level. The plateau was rediscovered in the fifties by Daniel Ruzo, an explorer who is more interested in the esoteric than in archaeology. This plateau has some geological anomalies that would turn out to be sculptures from an unknown protohistoric race. Ruzo calls this rock building civilization the Masma and connects them anthropologically with the Masmudas in northern Africa, the Atlanteans, and the Ten Lost Tribes of Israel.

Marcahuasi, like many other places with mysterious ruins, and many constructions in Cusco and the surrounding areas, shows evidence of a rock polishing or softening technique. These rocks have been altered to create megalithic sculptures, as well as walls, halls, and surface and subterranean tombs.

Marcahuasi and the Tayos both have the peculiarity that they revolve around a legend of a lost ancestral library, probably dated before the Flood, and both are subterranean.

In 1993 I went down to the Infiernillo (little hell) tunnel, a peculiar part of the plateau with a large crack or fissure that is 82 feet deep. I visited a place that had accumulated sediment for thousands of years and that contained the royal tomb where maidens were sacrificed in honor of the local deity, the god Wallallo. This same character is represented on the surface, looking to heaven, and he seems to have a helmet that makes him look very similar to the controversial face on Mars.

During my explorations in the Marcahuasi Ruins and the Tayos Caves, I felt the tragic presence of something unknown, something cursed, even diabolical, that had been brewing for centuries, hanging over the shoulders of the protagonists or pseudoauthors of a dual myth that keeps slipping through our fingers, devouring its participants and coming back to life every so many years, always casting a different light at the end of the multiple tunnels—real or imaginary—that confirmed them.

My friends, who had been essential for my search, had died before, during, and after my expeditions. I almost got myself, and my brave colleagues, killed. All this happened after almost thirty years of chasing the same golden ghost. But in spite of it all, there was something—and there still is—that transcends all explanations and that gives us a different notion of existence and of the box we put around our limitless reality.

The main protagonists of the tragedy were gone, leaving us orphans, debating between truth and lies. I didn't have a final answer to my question about whether Moricz had lied to Aguado, or if Aguado had lied to us, the idealists, the disciples of an enigma that helps create a new and hopeful view of the world. I didn't know if they had lied to themselves, or if they fervently believed in those experiences that bordered on the metaphysical that they had in 1968, or if this experience had been the product of a plan to get revenge on the Mormons, who wanted to take the supposed treasure for themselves.

This might have even been a plan they repeated in a similar way when Moricz recommended Aguado as the guide to take Hall and Armstrong to the depths of a cave he wouldn't have recognized himself, but that had some clues that could guide them to the chamber or sublevel that had the treasure.

13

The
Impossible Libraries

During the summer of 2011 I made a four-month trip to explore and film the heights and jungles of Peru and Bolivia, and I found a clue to the existence of the pre-Columbian metallic libraries. It was a matter of finding other clues that hinted at the existence of information deposits, of a certain form of writing, to verify or refute the legendary aspects of the Tayos, to find a final truth.

Javier Sierra wrote about my explorations in the magazine *Más Allá de la Ciencia* (Beyond science). He said, "The idea that in some remote spot of the planet, hidden under a mountain, or in the passages of a pyramid, the lost story of the origins of our species is hidden is an old and powerful archetype." This coincided with the Mormon doctrine that golden plates were the perfect media used by ancient civilizations to record their history.

Sierra wrote that my expeditions were "a step forward for that archetype of the lost library. I have the impression that in this case, like in the searches for the Holy Grail, the important thing is not reaching the goal, but continuing the search. The path, not fate, will teach us the lesson."

Sierra was one of the few authors who believed that finding

the halls and libraries was important. He knew they all hide clues to the truth of those protohistoric times that have been forgotten in the chronicles of our ancestors.

Two Bolivian friends, Antonio Portugal Arvirzu and Marcelo Saiduni, who are members of a group doing state-of-the-art archaeological studies with an emphasis on the Aymara culture, talked to me about a sixteenth-century book based on plates reconstructed from other, more ancient ones found on the islands of Lake Titicaca. This book mentions two hundred drawers with golden and silver plates, engraved stones, and slates filled with hieroglyphs with countless objects, all reflecting the high level of culture and civilization of these ancient people.

These manuscripts had been compiled by a sixteenth-century Augustinian priest, Brother Baltasar de Sales. He classified these materials found in tunnels that were similar to underground mining ducts, describing as them "hieratic and demotic plates and stones." In the Aymara language, these records were known as the *kkellkas* and *kipos*, which were later used by the pre-Incas and Incas. These "hieratic plates," made of thick, rustic materials, dated to two thousand years before the Flood.

At these sites Baltasar de Sales and his researchers also found sculptures that, like the plates, depicted humans, mountains, rivers, and land and sea monsters. Many of the recurring topics in the engravings showed Noah's Ark next to the sun, the moon, and the fixed stars. The year 2158 AM (or anno mundi, a calculation based on biblical accounts of the creation of the world) appears in some plates; this was the year of the death of Noah's son Shem.

In de Sales's book, the second age describes Hebrew plates and sculptures from 2530 AM, when the Israelites left Midian. These have representations of the tau, a T-shaped cross with a metal serpent. They also show the golden calf at the foot of Mount Sinai;

the IHS Christogram of the Jesuits; a tabernacle with cherubs, bells, and drawings; and sacred musical instruments.

These themes are mixed with Aymara symbols and legends, giving birth to the religious subculture of the *gentiles*,* who lived in the south and in the western Andean mountains, as well as in the north of Chile and Argentina.

De Sales also says there is a third age that is shown on sixteen divine plates whose motifs were the same as those symbols adored in the Middle East until 80 CE. The plates seem to have been made by the local natives under the influence of the Catholic priests and friars. De Sales's obscure book of the eighteenth century mentions a total of 111 talismans and oracles of the Incan Empire with hieroglyphs that cover the three ages. But the question remains: where are all these artifacts?

THE SACRED LINES TO THE ORIGIN

To find more answers, I decided to embark on another, smaller expedition to the place where it all began, where the Incas were supposed to have originated: Pacaritambo. Bernabé Cobo had described it in 1653, when the Spaniards had occupied and dominated the Peruvian mountains for over one hundred years. Later, in 1913, it was studied by George Eaton.

Over the years, adobe superstructures with stone walls thought to have been used by the pre-Incas, Incas, and Aymaras have been found. But about five generations later, scholars would find that here was the evident origin of the *ceque* system: lines that connected

---

*The gentiles have been the topic of recent expeditions and researches in the Andean deserts. It is interesting that archaeologists and anthropologists don't know or ignore the term, which is still used in many towns and regions. In Chile, the gentiles are tiny beings, but in Bolivia and Peru the term is used for giants and is linked to these through semisubterranean burials and *chullpas,* rectangular or circular funerary constructions used by pre-Incas and Incas, as well as other aboriginal cultures of the Andes.

pre-Incan and Incan sanctuaries, plazas, and native communities. In 1585, Juan Polo de Ondegardo had listed hundreds of these systems that "had to be destroyed."

The Jesuits had warned the Crown of this invisible but powerful network. Another regent, Cristobal de Albornoz (1582), had defined these ceque systems as "diabolical lines." In ancient Quechua they were called *checan ceque* or *direct consanguinity,* as well as *pallcarec ceque,* transverse or collateral lines, which meant that the lines were connected not only to the geography but also to the clans. The invisible power of the blood lineage was a secret and invisible language for the Spaniards, and the ignorance of the Spaniards never cracked the legacy and mystery of the Andean peoples.

One of these lines reached the Temple of the Moon, or the Palace of the Virgins of the Sun, in Coatí island in Lake Titicaca. These constructions had typical subterranean halls, and were made up of simple, interconnected rooms with multiple doorposts. This Coati temple overlaps with the creation myth of the pre-Inca, Inca, and Aymara, which states that the god Viracocha made the sun (analogous to the first Inca) and the moon (analogous to the first Coya, a name used for a mythical royal couple) emerge from Lake Titicaca.

In the sacred valley of the Incas, and to the southwest, where these cultures were born, we found huacas* of carved stones that corroborate these straight-line projections that go from Antisuyo to Chinchaysuyo. The directions of the lines were marked with the help of natural or man-made signs throughout the ceques—from three to fifteen—located as close as possible to the directions. These were considered sacred and have been called huacas since ancient times. The lines never crossed each other; they changed direction following a zigzag through the landscape and natural surroundings. Evidence of these lines is also confirmed by artifacts from the

---

*A huaca is a sacred aspect of the landscape.

Inca ritual of the Capac Cocha, ritual sacrifices performed on these sacred lines. The Inca priests traveled in a straight line visiting sanctuaries of the empire. These lines could and can be re-created from the vantage points toward the horizon, even with the confusion of the overpopulated city of Cusco. From Cusco, the cultural epicenter, the Incas moved in all directions.

Every myth begins with the original ancestors, who were gods or kings from mythical kingdoms. These original ancestors were born outside of the territory the elite group would later control. This appearance, or birth, outside of the dominated region, established the ancestral king and his descendants as foreigners. Anthropologists Graeber and Sahlins explain, "The governors don't even come from the same clay as the aboriginal people: they come from the Heavens, or from a different ethnic group. Royalty is always foreign."

THE CAVE OF ORIGIN

The pre-Incas and the Incas continued a more primordial system of following invisible lines that connect towns and sacred sites along the Andes. There is a very important association between solstitial sites and towns and religious or artistic sites, where we found constructions or stones or boulders with inscriptions.

The caves have always been a place of gestation. Thus, when we think of the Tayos, it is interesting to find connections with the ancestors of the Andean cultures. The gods created men in the depths of the oceans—where silence and darkness also reign—and in caverns and the depths of the Earth.

Manco Capac, the founding king of the Incas, went down to Cusco, fighting against his wife/sister, but he emerged from a cave east of Pacaritambo, 1.2 miles toward the hills known as Tamputoco or Tombotoco. The discoverer of Machu Picchu, Hiram Bingham III, passed through in 1912, but he did not describe the most important point. Manco Capac and the dynasty after him lived in Puma Orco, a sacred point. Legend talks about demigod ancestors of the Inca at Puma Orco, where the lines pass, protect, and radiate toward the south.

We have found pre-Inca ashlars along the south and northern Andes. These ashlars, which seem to have been made by being dissolved or softly sculpted, almost polished by hand, could soften and shape other granite or volcanic stones and were surrounded by circles and receptacles where water accumulated, working as a mirror for the sky.

It is said the internal chamber of these hill sanctuaries was used as an oracle by Manco Capac himself, and there was a niche as a window in one of the entrances. I could also observe—thanks to my young guide—the pool where Manco Capac's wife bathed; its edge was soft and curved.

Here began the mythical route of the founding Inca king. This pilgrimage road led to the Huanacaure sanctuary (close to Cusco), and then continued through the valley of the river to Yaurisque-Huaynacancha-Maukallaqta. Maukallaqta is newer than Puma Orco and is located on the Huaynacancha River. This region is a tributary of the Yaurisque River and on the other side of this river, there is an outcrop-sanctuary of the Purma Orco or Puma Orko.

The Spanish explorer Sarmiento de Gamboa talked about these regions and the legendary feats of the Inca Yupanqui Pachacuti. The same oracle existed in the town of Pacaritambo, with idols and stone statues. These sacred places are called *paqarinas*. Although these may have existed before Inca times, they developed fully under the Incan empire. According to Incan mythology, the creator god, Viracocha, ordered Manco Capac to emerge from the cave in Tamputoco.

THE MYSTERY OF THE NAME MANCO CAPAC

The name of the mysterious descendant of the sun and the moon, who became the first Inca, is fairly important. Mango or Manco is a name we also find in Mongolia; it is the name given by Marco Polo to Kublai Khan, brother of Genghis Khan. The Third Khan died in 1257, murdered in a place called Ho-Cheu (China), and he was succeeded by his second brother, Kublai, who took Tibet by storm. The Chinese pronounced the *g* very strongly, as in the word "bengal" that is also said "penkola." Yet it is interesting to note that ancient Peruvians had no *g* in their language, so it is not a stretch to say the *g* became a *c*.

There are other similarities between the ancient Mongolians and Incas. For example, the Incas and Mongolians both worshipped the same bird, the owl; in fact, the owl is said to have saved Genghis Khan's life.

In the portrait of the first Inca, Mango Capac, there is a representation of the sun, and over his armor-covered shoulder, a headpiece with sunrays. The exact time when the Mongolians started embellishing their weapons with the sun and the lion is not really known. It is also not known whether this had an astronomical interpretation, possibly with the constellation of Leo. In Taimingzing, in Mongolia, there are two cyclopean constructions shaped like an octagon, with large stone lions and turtles on each side. The lion symbol is common in Africa and is also represented by the cougar or leopard in North America and in several South American countries.

Beyond symbols, there are other similarities in names from the royalty or sovereigns of both kingdoms. For example, the Inca Pacha Camac, who was connected to the cult of the Sun and Earth, is the same name as a royal figure or sovereign of the Mongolians and Asians.

From the eighty-three languages of the American continent studied by the scholars Barton and Vater, 170 words are similar to those used by the Mongolians, or the Montchou, Tungouse, Samoyede, Tshoud, Biscayan, Coptics, and those in Congo.

According to the translations collected in Lican, the ancient capital of the Kingdom of Quito, the *quipos* or *quipus* were chosen by the

Puruays before defeating Manco Capac. Mongolian shares the words *quito, kito,* and *qipu.* The North American researcher and explorer John Ranking saw an interrelationship between the Mongolians and the Incan builders of Koricancha, the Temple of the Sun.

In the year 544, the Toltecas were eradicated from their own country, Huc Huc Tlopallan, and they arrived with seven leaders. They settled in Anahuac, where they built the city Tula, the most ancient city in America. A dynasty was founded in 670. There was a famine in 952, which caused another migration to Guatemala and Yucatán. The Tula is also a river in Mongolia; it flows through latitude 48—north of Ama. Legend says Quetzalcoatl walked with the Toltecas and a man called Kuthuku Lama and lived at Tula.

Ranking, who lived in the mid-nineteenth century, left behind many studies of the possible transmigrations from Asia to America. Unfortunately, his work has barely survived.

He was one of the few people to find evidence that the elephants arrived in America before the Conquest, in the thirteenth century, and he offers documents stating that the Mongolians brought them and rode on them to travel from Mexico to Peru.

He also rebuilds the story of the domestication of elephants fifty-eight centuries ago (thirty-five if you create your timeline based on the Deluge) by a culture previous to the Mongolians and the Huns. Only Herodotous talks about them, five centuries before the Common Era.

For 150 centuries the planet ignored the 180 degrees of latitude below the Equator, even if there was some knowledge of the east of Greenland in the Arctic Circle. But if we conclude that nothing was known in the south, under the Tropic of Capricorn, almost half the latitude was waiting to be discovered.

Ahead of many devotees of the wrongly named "fantastic realism," Ranking collected many stories of arches found in Europe and the United States. He was interested in the deposits found in the Ice Cave in California; in Fingal's Cave; and in the arch in the Arno valley in

Florence, where different species coexisted, such as hippopotamuses, rhinoceroses, elephants, oxen, horses, deer, hyenas, bears, tigers, wolves, mastodons, pigs, tapirs, and beavers. This was repeated all over the planet. Were there other Noahs who realized cataclysmic changes were coming and decided to safeguard the animals for the future, over two thousand years ago? The Muslim Mongolians of the fifteenth century did not suspect the convexity of the planet. If the canopy of the sky were a vase, or a container, and Earth were a string, and if calamities were arrows, and mankind the target of these arrows, and if the almighty god were the archer—though not a roaming one—then Adam's sons would surely find protection.

In the present period, much of the region in Africa between 10° north latitude and 30° south is blank for the civilized world. A large territory between Tibet and Siberia has been, and still is, imperfectly described. Half of the Earth has not been visited by people with the correct qualifications to communicate knowledge of civilizations, economics and trade, or history.

Timougin, Pisouca's son, the chief of the Mongolian tribe near the Baikal Lake in Siberia, was finally proclaimed Genghis Khan, or Grand Khan, in 1205 CE. Before the death of his grandson Kublai toward the end of the thirteenth century, the Asian continent was conquered. After the European consternation Japan was invaded, and as a consequence of that storm, the generals and troops that rose up escaped to reach America.

"When the Mongolians arrived," Ranking writes, "America was a wild territory. Suddenly, two empires were founded with the splendor, ceremony and greatness of the grand Asian sovereigns." When you travel and explore the Andes there is no doubt there is a heavy oriental influence.

Ranking believed Manco Capac was the son of the Great Khan Kublai and that Moctezuma was the ancestor of the great Mongolian of the Tangut region: Assam.

14

The Expedition to the Coangos River

"Trying to get to the Coangos is a sure way to die; you can go if you want to, but you must face the consequences on your souls," an old Shuar lady with a very wrinkled face told us without looking at our eyes. I suddenly had a sense of déjà vu, because four months before, I had lived a similar experience when I was abandoned by my filming crew and by a major from the Ecuadorian Special Air Forces. I had written this:

> I was in front of the Tayos Cave, and I had to take a step back because of the threat of a group of women and some of their furious husbands, who were standing on the edge of the bridge that goes over the Namangoza Gorge. This was the first of my tests, the first of the seven circles of hell I would have to face to reach my long-expected goal.

Paraphrasing Paulo Coelho, I sat down next to the river and cried. I had waited twenty-seven years for this moment, and now the cowardice of those who came with me conspired against my own creation. Even my own guide, Lucho Nivelo, who was not a Shuar, there considered not a native but a *colono,* a foreigner of European origin, was conspiring against me. I had one beer, then another one, until I noticed he started filming me. There I confess I felt like Andreas Faber-Kaiser: so close yet so far. Now more than ever, I understand his writings; I believe in his infernal voyage. I was suffering what you suffered, my dear Andreas.

I was facing the hardest challenge of my life. It was now or never. I was worried about the vertical descent of the main cave at the Coangos's river; which is why I had chosen the GIR, the Group of Intervention and Rescue, to help me. I knew they could help me reach my goal easily. But in spite of the great deception, I still had the option to go back north, to Morona-Santiago, and explore the area Stanley Hall said was the real Tayos Cave of the treasures.

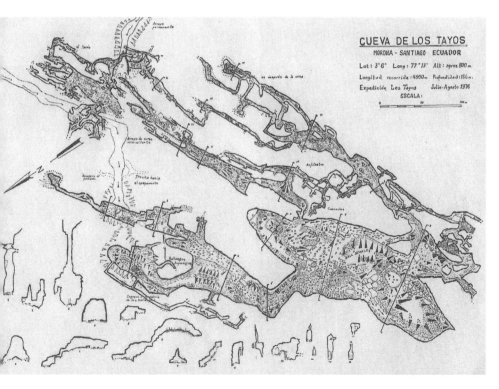

A map of the interior of the Coangos caves

IS THE THIRD TIME THE CHARM?

The incursions to the cave in Pastaza had been fruitful, but these were basilicas that led to the mother cathedral: the Tayos Cave. I was about to give up and postpone the final assault until after the rainy season (May or June). If this happened, I would have lost almost an entire year in Ecuador, observing the country struggle to keep a stable democracy, because the previous governments hadn't lasted long. One of the reasons for this was the enervation of the indigenous population of the area, which I was now beginning to experience in the flesh.

After patiently learning what waiting meant, I was able to make a third attempt to explore. This time I had the support of the GIR, who had trained me in mountaineering and survival on land, in the jungle, and in the water, and whom I invited to come with me. So two men joined my team, Ivan Jacome "Kleber" Rodriguez, who had Quechua ancestors and knew the east of the country, and Jorge Caicedo, an expert scuba diver—something that could be useful if the subterranean river had swollen enough to turn the floor of the cavern into a giant lake. (To see some members of my team, see plate 17.)

We started and got to Yuquianza. We sent our belongings on donkeys, and they would get there after we did. At least I had crossed the first bridge. The Namangoza Gorge was loud but peaceful, unaware of our fears and of the new storms being formed in the gray and green skies.

THE PETROGLYPHS OF HOPE

In La Esperanza (also called "The Hope," a small village composed of a bunch of wooden cabins, a school, and a soccer field), we arrived at a river and a rock engraved with petroglyphs. My friends from the GIR had a piece of chalk, with which they marked the ancient

Petroglyphs of La Esperanza

images. The old Jaia, a friend of Moricz's who lived in The Hope, told me that Moricz said those drawings were a map to Atahualpa's treasure. The images represented the animals of the area, such as amphibians and reptiles, but there were also other half-human, half-animal representations.

There we discovered the road was closed and the bridge was still destroyed. Moreover, the Shuar from La Unión wouldn't allow us to pass without the proper documentation from the Shuar center, Sucua, and without the authorization of their Darth Vader, Miguel Tancamash, the chief of the federation, who had given the order to stop and lynch anyone who dared pass without his permission. But my friends from the GIR were different from the people I had come with before, and before we left Quito they had sent me a message: "We will stay with you until the end."

At that moment, Nivelo, our guide, started having second

thoughts again. His nervousness validated the rumors that he wasn't welcome in those places, which were true even if I refused to believe them. Another déjà vu, because he had done the exact same thing to me the previous November.

It was getting late, and La Unión was a couple of hours away. By the time we got there it would be dark, and those places, in spite of the innocent energy of the jungle, would become inhospitable. Anything could happen; the jungle has a thousand eyes, many of which don't have a conscience.

Rain started pouring down while the members of the GIR played soccer with children and young men in the central square. Night fell, and it would be loud, thanks to the karaoke not far away at the little school. Thunder could be heard until late at night, and it became confused with the violent messages from the Shuar radio. Echoes of bitterness and grudges transmitted through the air, reminding me of what it would have been like to be in communist China.

Our guide came with the morning, the same man who the previous night had said the road was closed, and a lurking presage affected all of us.

The three members of the GIR were looking at me with disappointment and distress. Nivelo reappeared suddenly with Jaia, and with his face in a panic he said he was not going to continue with us; he was going to abandon us. The story was repeating itself. When I was forgiving his dubious acts from months before, in my first expedition, he was acting the same way again. Kleber and Caicedo, the guys from my support team, went to confer far from me. The sky was half gray, half light blue. Although flashes of panicked anguish went up to my throat, I said to myself: I will continue alone. When they came back from their powwow in a corner of the dusty soccer field, I knew what they were going to say: better if we leave and return again with better permits and more support. But I had my answer ready: "I'm not retreating. If you don't want to continue with me, I will go alone, and hire help on the way, or in the last town."

Kleber said that I was his and their responsibility, as they had confirmed with their commander before our departure from Quito. A few minutes later, we were packing the horses and mules and strapping the heavy generator over one of the beasts (see plate 18).

This is how I came to be reunited with Lucho Chamin, who told us that the night before he had had a dream in which a child asked him if he knew how many birds there could be in the Tayos Cave, and that he had to go with him. Maybe that child was me. So Lucho "the Shaman" Chamin agreed to come with us to the border of the Zamora River, our second circle of hell.

In the direction to another crisscross of rivers, La Unión, where the Santiago River originates from the convergence of the Zamora River with the Namangoza,* a mysterious figure appeared, another farmer. I was surprised by the tattoos on his chest and arms; a giant Templar cross covered his naked torso. I smiled at Kleber, who had been asking about the Knights Templar. He said that even though he was Ecuadorian, he felt he had been one of them.

At the other side of the river, a group of Shuar leaders came to see us in the distance. One of them was holding a small-caliber rifle, as I saw through my zoom lens. The only way of crossing was through a pulley or *tarabita,* a kind of suspended basket.

Despite his resistance I sent Kleber, who has Indian blood from a nearby region, to negotiate with the committee. I had a feeling that I was in the Wild West.

---

*The Santiago River originates from the union of the Namangoza and Zamora Rivers in the province of Morona-Santiago, in the northern part of the Cóndor mountain range, almost on the border between Peru and Ecuador. The Namangoza is an Ecuadorian river that originates from the confluence of the Paute and Negro Rivers. The Santiago River runs just thirty-four miles in Ecuadorian territory until it reaches the border with Peru, where the river turns south.

Kleber came with pessimistic news. We needed federal permission. The business card of the tribal representative in the capital (a Mr. Champi) was not enough. I decided to send Kleber again with Lucho, who was going to emphasize that I had already talked for several months with the proper authorities, and to wait, with extreme patience, for a letter of authorization.

Offering money, and a possible donation of the brand-new generator, was the opening of this second circle of green hell.

There we crossed, leaving Lucho behind, as he couldn't continue with us, although he promised to rejoin us on the return way when we passed through La Esperanza.

We crossed. We stayed overnight. At night, there was electricity all around the camp. When I went to the bathroom, better known as the bushes, I saw some weird lights, like mercury lamps, moving behind the trees. At first I thought it might be lightning moving south, but I was wrong: the lights were very close. Suddenly they disappeared into the night, and I decided to continue on my own in spite of it all.

AT LONG LAST: TAYOS

Finally the jungle roads, red mud, and swampy rain were opening. (For photos of the area, see plates 19 and 20.)

The heavy storm proved that we were still at the end of the rainy season. Just when all was looking better and I was feeling confident again, the muddy path started to slow our uphill climb. Our boots, like the horse carrying the generator, sank deep. Once in a while my feet came out from my rain boots along the path. The GIR guys were leaving me behind, and the stress started to accumulate. After almost six months of waiting, paperwork, cross-cultural meetings with bureaucrats and the circles of power in the sierra and the jungle, the horse was falling. Damned rain. Why not wait for another day of sunshine and butterflies?

The village of Coangos was slowly showing its scattered wood and straw housing, its small grass center, and, in the distance, the foggy hills, where the caverns were waiting.

The community leaders came to receive us; meanwhile, we rested our heavy equipment in a porch of one of the surrounding cabins. Again I received a negative response. I offered the 1500-watt Yamaha generator as a password to my target. I also experienced an instant of happiness, knowing I was the first to bring electricity to a town that didn't have any way to illuminate itself, and especially to the school.

The fatigue was overcoming me again, but I activated the camera. I had to record when I donated the generator, as evidence. But every time I tried to photograph the children, they slipped away. They both wanted and did not want to be captured.

The trustee and the teacher of the school, Luis, had to decide whether we would be given permission today. The boys of the GIR were in a hurry, since they only had five days allocated for this mission. In addition, the patrol car was to return from the bridge and hostel of Huichanza on Saturday afternoon. Furthermore, the original permission from the members of La Unión was only to stay one day in the caves. Both the *comuneros* of that locality and those of Coangos agreed that the access would be brief, that they would help us to arrive at the place, and that two of them would supervise. Later on I would realize that they were taking the advantage of my party's presence to hunt tayos.

We left that afternoon. At noon the next day we arrived at Coangos, reaching a river that was narrower and calmer than the Zamora. There the road went down and down, and then it went up a little, and there it was emerald green. It drizzled. I almost cried with emotion. I could barely see the cave's mouth—a gap between black and dark—my longed-for moment at the threshold of the Cueva de los Tayos.

I couldn't believe I was going down and that I would be walking through the Tayos Cave. Moricz's, Aguado's, and Hall's cave . . . a cave that had belonged to the Shuar for centuries.

As I was going down, the climbing rope made me twirl slightly. I kept going down, and pressing the descent device for what felt like an eternity. It was still drizzling, and soil and small rocks fell with the rain, going down with me. It was one of the most exciting experiences of my life, going down to the mother's womb, the Ecuadorian Pachamama, the sacred interior of the cathedral of stone, the cave of Coangos.

When I looked up, the image was still spectacular. The sun's rays created a trail that highlighted soil particles floating on the air. It reminded me of the afternoons in my childhood bedroom, where I imagined galaxies and universes in each speck of dust illuminated by the sun coming through my window.

On the other end of the first plaza, a large hole opened, and we had to go down 23 feet to a second level. Here we would find an almost perfectly rectangular portal under which one has to crouch to enter, leading to a tunnel that is symmetrical from its entrance to its exit. During the 1969 expedition it was baptized von Däniken's Arch, although it was rebaptized as Moricz's Arch after von Däniken fell into disrepute. Some 164 feet from the descent area, we found the first slope or descent of less than 33 feet. We decided to continue down to this level. There was the arch and the tunnels with vitrified walls—two of the parts of the cave I considered to be the most important. (To see interior images of the caves, see plates 21, 22, and 23.)

I filmed the entrance, and from there I concentrated on the tunnel rising to our left and above me, the one with the polished ceiling. The GIR guys went in with me. We passed through the arch into Stanley Hall's Gallery, where we heard thousands of tayos cawing.

The floor was unstable, loose, and muddy, and it crackled as we walked. This, as we discovered, was due to the seeds and little tayos eggs that cover the natural carpet of the cave surface (see plate 24). It was a naturally yellowish tan that emitted a phosphorescent greenish aura, something out of a novel by Jules Verne (see plate 25). This was the product of the blind birds, which unknowingly carry parts of the outside flora in their feathers into and out of the cave.

We continued west, under a giant vault. It was the first part of Stanley Hall's Gallery. As we continued forward, I found the formation of perfectly cut stones, like a petrified loaf of bread forming a dome. Since I had already seen the photos of the 1969 expedition, I was intrigued to see and touch those cyclopean artifacts. The more rational analysts believe they are pieces of rock that have been detached from the giant vault above us. But there is no visual evidence that these rocks fell from the ceiling; the rocks seem to have been moved and piled this way on purpose.

We continued west for several miles through the cave, until we reached a rocky plaza with sides that curved in a semicircle or amphitheater. As it bent east, the floor descended, making us slide and run into some bird's nests made of straw and mud, which seemed to have fallen from above. We were in the stalagmite zone.

It didn't take me long to recognize the place that the English had named "the ladder" thirty years before (see plate 26 showing stone steps). These stone steps went down to other galleries on several levels. This was the point of convergence with what seemed to be the Commando Cave. As we descended to another level, we found a smaller room with perfectly polished ceilings and walls, like passageways opening to the left and over the entrance to the second gallery. From there we walked through the monoliths, where we camped. Here the Shuar guides invited us to a dinner of tayos, which they had caught and cooked.

While the GIR guys slept, I ventured with difficulty to continue my search for two sculptures I had heard about at the Serbian cultural center in November. One was a sculpture a Belgian man tried to rip from the stone—it resembled a chalice or baptismal font—and the other one represented a dove or the Holy Spirit. These images were connected more to Christianity than to Shuar pantheism.

One of the Shuar said he knew what I was talking about, so both of them took me up to the forest of stalactites and stalagmites, where Neil Armstrong's picture was taken (recall page 166). In this jungle of limestone obelisks, I discovered petroleum flowing through the cave. I started feeling tired again; my legs wouldn't move anymore. I told the two Shuar that we should go back. On the way back I found a strange lateral chamber I was tempted to explore. I felt this place could have been ideal for hiding a library, since it reminded me of the Infiernillo or Little Hell of Marcahuasi. The Shuar were staring at each other. They didn't want to go in with me. I felt they knew something I didn't, and that the chamber was forbidden to them, or maybe they had seen something there in the past. I would have liked to continue, but I saw another opening on the subsoil, and I would need a lot of time to explore a second sublevel.

When I returned, my friends were awake. It was time to go back, but I would have liked to film the sunrise in Hall's Chamber (where the picture of a giant supported the old legends that they had lived in these caves). But for this I would have to wait until after six, and the men from GIR had to help me climb those thirty-three feet of slippery walls.

As we retraced our steps, I saw von Däniken's Arch and discovered the famous angular stone that had always been with me since Aguado showed me the picture in 1997 as evidence of human work in that portal and in the Tayos Cave. This simple stone was evidence enough. This technique would be copied in the megaliths and in the European cathedrals, and it didn't need a compass or a square.

The upper angle of the left side was identical to the one on the right side. Eureka! This was the angular stone that held the large rectangular slab of von Däniken's Arch. This was symmetry that could not be attributed to Mother Nature or to any kind of erosion (see plate 27).

The return to the main hall was difficult, but we managed it. The ascent took us almost eight hours. I was second to go down and second to last to go out (see plate 28).

ESCAPE FROM THE THREE RIVERS OF THE CIRCLE OF HELL

I didn't realize there was any suspicion from the guys who had helped us. Maybe the owner of the cave wanted a reward. I was so tired that everything felt like a dream, but the feeling of coming out baptized lingered in me. I preferred not to think, I didn't have the strength to keep on taking pictures or filming, even if I had promised Caicedo I would try to register the descent. I found out that two other Shuar had stayed to stand watch during our ascent, because the GIR feared they would cut our ropes at night, as had happened before. They weren't wrong.

We were on our way to Coangos again. Kleber was still worried we wouldn't get there on time, and he planned to go ahead. We would return to Coangos, and from there we would get to La Unión to spend the night on the same ranch. The next day we would cross using the cable cars over the Zamora to get close to Huichanza.

I was going on horseback, and we were going to meet at the ranch where we left the equipment that was too heavy. Among these things I had left my White's 1500 metal detector, which was ideal for locating large areas of gold. My GIR comrades went ahead of me, taking the other workhorse with the cameras and instruments.

The night was falling. We could barely see the path. There was more mud and mosquitoes, more venomous than before. Suddenly a young man intercepted us, saying that Kleber had almost been killed before reaching the Zamora River. They had hidden him in a cabin, because there were other gangs, a total of ten Shuar, who had come from four different communities to kill us.

I smelled death in the air, like a fine and cold dagger. I felt the karma and the curse of the Tayos saga on my skin and on my conscience. Maybe my time had come, and I didn't know if I deserved the luck of the previous explorers and researchers. Or maybe I did, and I would soon meet Moricz, Aguardo, Jaramillo, and Faber-Kaiser on that side of this diabolical story.

A Shuar woman saved Kleber and then us. We were in a small crowded room. The GIR guys were furious that they had listened to me. This is where I found out the Austrian nine-millimeter guns hadn't been left behind; they still had them.

We had to remain quiet, without making a sound or turning on a light. The barrack had many holes through which light was shining, but I didn't know if this light was from the lightning from the storm or from the torches of the angry Shuar, who had a license to kill us. Two weeks before, they had burned another Shuar alive for trafficking in and exporting *Tzantzas,* the shrunken heads that were sold for thousands of dollars on the black market.

I thought that night would never end. I prayed to Father Crespi. He had been a part of this story, and since he was being sanctified, maybe he could send us some of his peace. If we had had a confrontation, we would have endangered the family that was sheltering us. Suddenly someone was shooting at our heads. At the other side of the wall, the children of our protector started crying when their mother yelled, "They're coming!" The dogs were barking. The lightning continued, but the men weren't getting any closer.

My GIR friends started to become very tense, especially Caicedo, who was my main recriminator. We were crowded in a small space, and fear was in the air. Caicedo starting blaming me again while kicking me a couple of times with his boots. I felt his sweat and fury as he said, "For your cause we are going to die!" Kleber and Caicedo were more restrained, but they too reminded me that we should have left earlier and that I had prolonged my stay in the caves. I was calm, relaxed, but also anguished, begging to the universe that nobody be hurt because of me and my expedition. I had been waiting for such a long time, but the sacrifice of all those years was not worth the loss of the life of anyone, especially the young and innocent family in the next shack.

Suddenly a cloak of silence covered the humid night, but I still felt and smelled the torches, and maybe the alcohol on the attackers around us.

We decided to leave most of the equipment and get to the river to try to cross in the cable car before being detected. Our savior, the Christian Shuar woman who helped us, said that we should leave at five in the morning, because at that time our pursuers would still be sleeping off the alcohol they had drunk at night.

So at five o'clock, before the rooster could crow, we slipped off through a ditch that used to be the drainage of an old path. We couldn't see much, but in fifteen minutes we reached the crossroads. We had help from the men, the Shuar woman, her son, and two grandchildren. When we crossed the torrential Zamora, which had never before looked so black, we heard people on our tracks. We disabled the cable car so they couldn't cross. All we heard were some distant insults.

On the other side of the descent to the river, we found the place where they had planned to ambush us the night before. Dozens of footsteps and cartons of cheap wine attested to the macabre wait.

"Run for your life, Alex!" My colleagues repeated over and over. I don't think I've ever run so fast. Dawn was rushing upon us. It was a half hour of terrible ascent, with the risk of falling on the sides or of putting a hand on a venomous snake. Breathless and completely heated up, without even having to drink ayahuasca, we reached the bridge of the Namangoza Gorge.

We feared there would be another ambush on the Yuquianza, but there wasn't. A smiling Lucho, the shaman, was waiting for us with the other officer from the Coangos. They were there to help us in case of any more trouble. The worst was over.

I had made it. I had conquered the Tayos Cave. I had walked on the tightrope of a curse that will still live in me until I can determine whether Moricz and Aguado were telling the truth—had they seen what they swore they had seen, or was it all a vision from another spiritual search that had been born down there, a long time ago? Was it the result of material and intellectual greed? The dream of El Dorado has no limits.

Who was I to judge them or the Shuar? That night I forgave my enemies, even if I hadn't seen their faces and didn't know their names or how to pronounce them. I had forgiven them without really knowing them. Maybe because they could end my dream, end my almost thirty years of doubts, of dreams, of feverish dwelling between the protohistoric and the stellar. Who was I to pretend to know the secret of the centuries? Another link in the chain of desperation. I was ahead of many, and in that edge of the abyss I didn't understand many things, with the exception of one provable thing. What? I had found myself.

A TENTATIVE HYPOTHESIS: FINDING A FINAL EXPLANATION

Many friends have asked me why I haven't come to a conclusion. I have come to many conclusions. I have been awoken in the middle of the night, holding the key of what happened several times, and because I didn't write it down, I lost it again when I went back to sleep. This is a little bit of a metaphor, but a little bit true. In spite of my friendship with some of the characters, who might have introduced me to this topic from a subjective point of view, I have left aside nostalgia and the unavoidable favoritism to find a final approach.

I think Petronio Jaramillo Abarca picked up Shuar legends he heard as a child, and after assimilating them, being the incipient man of letters he was, he absorbed them as his.

Moricz was in the process of searching for something when he heard the story from Andrés Fernández Salvador Zaldumbide, and later he heard that same story from the group that hung out with Jaramillo in Quito, with Alfredo Moebius, so he used the story to corroborate the theory that it was fate guiding him.

Moricz had more information than just the coincidence of the sacred bird in his family's coat of arms. He had knowledge, and he was a visionary of the hypogeum, of the subterranean. His time with the Cayapa (colored) Indians and his incursions in the Achuar-Shuar territory connected him to the Jíbaro cosmogony, which was probably the complete opposite of the Indo-European shamanism he had synthesized in a theosophical Europe, in the Hungarian land that saw him grow. It is possible that he had teachers connected to the Ahnenerbe (a Nazi Germany think tank), but without any documents to prove this, we can't assert it was actually true.

It is possible these Achuar-Shuar sacred sites have subterranean portals or doors to parallel universes. This might be why they have a tradition of hallucinogenic plants and of living in a state of unreality, a culture of a Buddhist-like *maya* that is beyond good and evil, between creation and destruction.

The shaman descendants who guided Moricz don't know anything of the whereabouts or of the existence of a metallic library in the area of Morona-Santiago. They do remember that the Jíbaros used to decorate trees and caves with metal plates they drew on and cut, and more recently these were made of brass, but they don't remember a gigantic library like those from the stories, which claim that they exist on the physical plane.

It is possible that Julio's and Moricz's experiences were induced by one of these special places, and this experience was similar to the one the Jíbaros told Jaramillo about in the fifties. But there is also another Tayos Cave, far away from the one in the Coangos River, closer to the Yaupi River, and this one might hold one of the keys.

Moricz mentioned several times, especially in the sworn declaration of 1969, that the treasures were scattered across several Tayos Caves, not just in one. This would confirm Jaramillo's story, which had taken place hundreds of miles from the caves of the expeditions in 1969 and 1976.

15

Psychic Archaeology and the Tayos Mystery

Decades ago the U.S. government developed a program called "remote viewing" for its intelligence and military branches.

This program was developed by two physicists and a small group of psychics; its leader was the artist and parapsychology researcher Ingo Swann. Swann coined the term *remote viewing*, and he perfected this technique, which uses the longitudes and latitudes of our planet. It is a sort of invisible, transcendental mathematical technique that follows the universal laws both of the natural sciences and of what cannot be measured by our senses.

Unfortunately, from the Cold War up to our days, remote viewing has slowly degenerated because of the use that has been made of it in psychic espionage. This technology was at first monopolized by different government departments, which believed in the results confirmed between the seventies and the nineties.

Even if psychic archaeology existed before remote viewing, it was never developed as a discipline independent from the clairvoyants who created it.

Professor Norman from Toronto University was lucky enough to meet George McMullen, a psychic from British Columbia who not only helped find many aboriginal sites in Canada but also participated in international expeditions. One of them had to do with the discovery of the sunken palace of Cleopatra and Mark Antony along the coast of Alexandria. McMullen also participated in the search for the tomb of Alexander the Great, and he described in great detail the possible location of the remains of the Pharos (lighthouse) of Alexandria.

I had the opportunity to meet and test him when I was looking for an Atchumawi ceremonial site in Modoc County in northeast California. Thanks to his guidance, I was able to find the ceremonial stone circle. My partner at the time had been looking for this site since she had left the territory as a little girl. Her grandmother used to tell her stories of the healing ceremonies that took place in that circle and of the sacred waters visited by the Modoc and Pit River tribes every year. After studying the data, I found in the middle of a forest a nearly oval-shaped circle with vertical standing slabs that gave the feeling of a prehistoric tomb site.

Years later I started thinking I could use the help of psychics and remote viewers as a second option to the physical search of the lost treasure of the metallic library. I wanted to ask McMullen to use a map of Ecuador to find new clues to a new discovery or to confirm the Tayos mystery's already existing clues. Unfortunately, the maps I had with me did not have the geographic precision he required, and when I got my hands on the sort of map he needed, I could not locate him in the west coast of Canada, where he lived. When I tried again, he had already passed away.

One psychic who helped me was none other than Ingo Swann, an unforgettable friend and mentor for many years until his death. Swann did not agree very often to probe or put his system to the test. But I told him about the Tayos mystery. Over the years I gave him and his best disciples the coordinates so they could help me, both when Ingo was alive and after his unexpected death.

The first one to help me was Robert Duran, who had been recently trained by Swann. (For over a decade Swann refused to train new candidates who couldn't stand the cost of his training. It was not exorbitant, like some of the trainings today, but it was very exhausting.) Duran performed some experimental readings that matched the geography I would face a couple of years later. In our sessions, we discovered that along a river there were triangular or sagittal-shaped cuts over the land or coastal border. These cracks interpenetrated, like vertices that lined a "V" of inverted triangles.

When I reached that river (the Pastaza), I could not spot these formations. They were not in plain sight or hidden, but I believed these entrances opened to a subterranean chamber near the entrance of a Tayos cave system. This was near the latitude of the new Stanley Hall cave, which, according to Hall, was also Jaramillo's cave.

Swann had also told Duran to continue the remote-viewing practice with me and to help me use the system for archaeological detection and solving the mysteries of the past. One of the first objectives of the remote-viewing program was espionage, both geopolitical and industrial. It could also be used to go back to the past or find lost artifacts, so I found it fascinating and believed it was capable of reviewing and solving historical or archaeological mysteries.

So I continued my search. The next step was to ask Paul Smith, the founding partner of the IRVA (International Remote Viewing Association) to help me. Swann always spoke highly of him and even gave me his phone number.

When I got in touch with Smith, I told him about my decade-long search. He found it interesting because he was also a Mormon. When I got in touch with him, he had just moved to Utah, the home of the church of the Latter-day Saints.

My patience was running short after months of waiting, because Smith needed to use a student from one of his yearly classes. Remote viewers had recently become money-making machines, for industrial espionage in particular. They were the new private investigators of the mind.

After talking to a couple of candidates, Smith finally found one who was available. This one ended up describing a semisubterranean nuclear rocket base. Smith ruled him out, because he had also studied the topic and used the system over the same latitudes and longitudes in question. After changing students, Smith determined they were not ready to help me with my task, so he focused on one student who gave us a random and confusing message. This is what Smith answered after several months of waiting:

> My viewer made one more try at your cave. The session results had nothing about a cave or gold or records in it (in fact, far from any of that). Yet another session the viewer did around the same time against a target I knew was real-world was spot-on. He did an awesome job on it. That increases my conviction that there is nothing to the cave account that remote viewing can do. Not conclusive evidence, but enough for me. I'm not going to pursue this again.

So I was left alone again with my mystery, facing the danger of falling into a cloud of noise and confusion, as happens when one penetrates the worlds of the subconscious and the paranormal, of ancestral forces and energies. I was not satisfied with the viewer Smith had used. First he described a nuclear base with nuclear silos and rockets, something that was as unlikely in the Ecuadorian jungle of the past as it was today.

Even so, I did not give up and still hoped to find a viewer who was more conscious or efficient than the others. The next one I spoke to had started gaining popularity and came highly recommended by a friend from the IRVA. He had Chilean relatives, but he did not speak Spanish. I still felt he was honest and eager to collaborate and help us solve the mysteries of the world.

It took him a couple of days to confirm that the metallic library did exist, but it was beyond the domain of the dimensional vortices or the doors to parallel worlds.

According to this viewer, the metallic library could be explored every couple of years or decades, when the circumstances provided a sort of "combined art," to use the term of the medieval Mallorcan philosopher Ramon Llull. Only those specific conditions would allow the explorer to find and see it for a limited time, within a specific space.

THE VOICE OF THE SPIRITS

I started thinking that traditional mediums could connect to Moricz and Aguado, but I wasn't thrilled with this idea.

Even so, one cold and snowy winter afternoon, I was in the house of a father and son who were mediums, and I could see how they struggled to connect to Aguado and Moricz. Right away they described the two men to me and told me Aguado liked to dress well. According to them, he looked as if he had had severe health and behavior issues in his early infancy.

Aguado was the fastest one to reach and would not yield to the presence of a skeptical and defensive Moricz. They were angry with each other. They said I already knew the truth and asked why I was still questioning it. I honestly didn't know any truths, and even today I question both their final testimonies, even if Aguado was such a good friend to me.

According to the mediums, Aguado was under the influence of Moricz, and Moricz was more than a father figure for him, even though Aguado was only twenty years younger. During the sessions the spirits didn't want to answer, and they started criticizing each other, saying they had broken the pact of silence.

Those of us within the Tayos circle and who had frequented the Argentinian Center for Speleology in those decades knew that Aguado had sworn that he would always obey every order and wish of the Hungarian explorer. In the interview in this book in chapter 7, Aguado confirms this statement.

Years later, in Los Angeles, I met a beautiful psychic who came from El Salvador and who was highly recommended. After I had dinner with her, she connected with my thoughts on Moricz and Aguado and concluded they had been scammers. Everything had been a scam to get money: they used the idea of the golden library to find funding to explore real gold mines in the area.

Another psychic detective to whom I showed pictures of the two men agreed they had been scammers, but it was all Moricz's idea. Aguado had agreed to the plan, and both were stuck in an irreversible situation. This was the view that many skeptics had voiced when they saw no hints of the treasure and started thinking the stories had no tangible truths behind them.

This psychic said Aguado had come up with the idea and had sent Moricz to Ecuador, and the latter, in spite of his metaphysical and spiritual searches, was hoping for a stroke of luck to find what he had lost in Central Europe.

I really cannot say remote viewing was effective because those who use it have probably gotten involved in the pragmatism behind it and cannot see beyond.

Previous experiments with gifted psychic archaeologists, as they were called thirty years ago, yielded better results.

Ingo Swann said we had to break the box of reality to be able to see, to see from the present to the past and to the future.

Most of the viewers I invited to help me, both veterans and beginners, agreed that the latitudes and longitudes of the two main caves of the metallic library had no tangible treasures in them.

Today, thanks to new technologies such as the Light Detection and Radar (LIDAR) system, we can easily and quickly confirm a rumor of a deposit or burial under the Amazon or African jungles, or in the high peaks of the Andes or European Alps.

As an example, I can mention my good friend Steve Elkins, who searched for the White City by land for a couple of decades and never found what was also known as the Lost City of the Monkey God in the Mosquitia region of Honduras.

The myths and legends of the indigenous population and the explorers talked about an advanced city that was very similar to those of the Mayas. Elkins preferred to use science, not intuition; yet something made him continue his search, and he accomplished his goal when he discovered a very ancient, supposedly proto-Mayan city that had universal symbols also found in Indo-European cultures.

In short, the use of psychic archaeologists is not that necessary for locating sites, but it undoubtedly will continue being a way to determine if others are telling the truth.

Even so, we hope we can find new inventions to link the mind with remote perception, such as the electronic one used by new remote viewers.

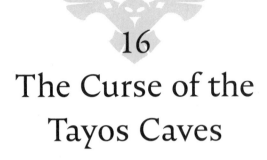

16

The Curse of the Tayos Caves

Some have spoken of the curse over the Tayos that is said to fall over those who dare venture into Shuar territory and into the metallic library.

The truth is that foreign forces have been lurking from the start and have deflected the objective of several explorers.

Just like those who have pilgrimaged around the world finding alternatives for the Holy Grail, the perspectives of the search for a "self" and the manifestation in the physical plane of the contents and symbols of the invisible started to take mysterious shapes.

One of the first victims was Samakache, who guided Pino Turolla to a river that lead to the location of the caves, which was probably the hill known as Cerro Blanco. The cacique, who was in poor health, crossed the torrential river first, lost his balance while jumping from rock to rock, and cut his thigh with his machete.

Back in populated territory, Samakache's wound became infected, and in spite of Turolla's care, he died in his arms. The person who said he knew the exact location of the Tayos Cave and had access to that subterranean world and the chamber with metallic plates died tragically.

In 1991 Juan Moricz died from a heart attack at the Continental

Hotel, it is said as the result of a lack of potassium. The waiter who found him said it looked as if his heart had exploded, because his torso was reddened with a visible colored spot in his chest.

Moricz's inseparable friend, Julio Goyén Aguado, was in the middle of an expedition to search for and extract mummies from the high peaks of the Malargue area in Mendoza, Argentina, when he suffered an unexpected accident. The truck in which several members of the Argentinian Center for Speleology were traveling lost control on a dirt road next to a cliff and fell over the precipice. Aguado was thrown out of the car, and as the truck fell, it crashed against his chest. The blow broke his ribs. It seemed he survived that impact, but panic accelerated his heart rate and caused a heart attack.

Years before, Andreas Faber-Kaiser, known for his work on ancient astronauts and contemporary conspiracies, tried to get to the Tayos Caves on his own. Moricz did not help him at all. After going several days through the jungle, tired and tormented, Faber-Kaiser reached the entrance of the cave, but a sudden fear stopped him from going down.

Years later, Faber-Kaiser died of AIDS, convinced that German intelligence had artificially infected him with that virus. To his dying day, he insisted that the Bayer pharmaceutical company was behind his sickness and demise.

Another, less important character was Gastón Fernández Borrero, the military man and tourism officer who helped Moricz organize the first formal expedition to the Coangos caves. One night some thieves broke into his house and found him while he was studying his Tayos photo archive for a book he was preparing. They hit him over the head and killed him.

But the most dramatic and unlikely victim was Petronio Jaramillo Abarca. He lived in Esmeraldas, and one day, after his classes at the university, he had dinner with his elder son and daughter-in-law. After the meal, while having some drinks, Jaramillo started making advances toward his son's wife. His son stabbed him and threw him in a ditch near his house.

Some people deny this version of the story. In 2009 I visited Esmeraldas to try to reconstruct the last days of one of the creators of the legend of the Tayos Cave.

The police confirmed that Jaramillo's son had killed him. He had been arrested and was still doing time in a prison in Ecuador. I also searched for other witnesses, but to find one of them I had to venture into the red-light district. I asked a policeman to accompany me to the entrance of this neighborhood, but the officer did not dare to enter it. "If you want, you can venture in, but I can't help you; you'll be doing this at your own risk." After walking for a few blocks I heard screaming and dogs barking, and I noticed the situation could get very dangerous in this labyrinth of alleys, so I went back to safety.

Stanley Hall denied this version of the story of Jaramillo's death, and he ended up supporting and protecting the youngest son, who had also been implicated in his father's murder and had to flee. Hall helped him get to Scotland and sheltered him for some time.

What can we infer from all these victims? Were their deaths a coincidence, or was there a causal link? Maybe there existed, and still exist, some guardians of the invisible outside or inside the caves.

The Shuar who guided Jaramillo and Moricz are long gone; only their sons remain, like Cajeke, the elder Shaman who teaches the religion and tradition of the Shuar. His culture still honors the traditions of his ancestors, but he does not remember his father (also named Cajeke) ever speaking of things that they had to guard, fear, or venerate in the depths of the caves.

As many have experienced the presence of beings that have been seen and even recorded once, we must believe there are several life forms within the Tayos cave system. I remember that Aguado used to say that "with the correct permits" we could enter the metallic library chamber.

When I reached the caves in the Pastaza and Coangos Rivers, the dwellers didn't know much about the legend that had created such in impact in the west. In the depths of the Amazon the tribes had no traditions of metallic plates.

We must read between the lines, thinning out the nonsense that has been spread online about the supernatural aspects of and conspiracies around the caves.

Moricz and Aguado never shared the physical location of the lost treasure. They kept silent in many interviews, and apocryphal articles said the site had been sealed. They said one of the passages leading to the chamber had been blown up after they received messages that mankind was not ready for such a discovery.

The Shuar-Achuar can teach us a spiritual lesson: if we are patient and we respect this foreign land, this place leads us to a new dreamlike stage, which changes when we change time, and when time changes, the space is also disrupted.

The Shuar live in a world different from ours. Still, upstream of the Pastaza River, the wise men couldn't tell me anything. They did not remember the plates, although they did remember hanging metal mirrors reflecting the sun. Other times they found metal plates affixed to trees. These plates had no writing on them and served as offerings of some kind. The venerable Sharupi had no memory or knowledge of the plates having any writing or ideographic signs in them.

There was no evidence aboveground on the surface of the rivers, and under them there were no special discoveries. It was almost like a silence coming from the depths that hushes all those who have dared enter the utter darkness of the caves, hoping to find something transcendental that others missed, failed to see, imagined, or lied about.

The truth is still down there, but I doubt we will be able to find natives or settlers who witnessed the events and who can give us the key to open the final revealing or condemning door.

The Tayos Manifesto

Because of the importance of the subject in my life, and because it is impossible to be with all of you, I have decided to write this manifesto. Although few are left of the first generation of explorers, the issue has endured and grown in an unexpected way.

Despite the negativity with which certain people and vested interests obstruct human progress, the word *no* does not exist in my vocabulary. You who are reading about my experiences should not accept the *no* of others, when you know deep within you that there is always another alternative, and that this does not depend on ignorance or on economics alone.

The French poet Paul Éluard's statement—"There are other worlds, but they are in this one"—continues to resonate with me. Another is, "on the cosmic scale only the fantastic tends to be reality"—the famous statement of Pierre Teilhard de Chardin, who tried to unite anthropology and the natural sciences with the spiritual and asserted the evolution of the physical toward the spiritual.

A new generation, which is already on the planet and which will reach its apogee over the remainder of the century, may be able to understand what earlier explorers began toward the last quarter of the twentieth century.

Maybe there is a message from the Tayos—writing that could be on metals that are no longer part of this dimension but that we can reach through higher states of consciousness. And advanced beings from those depths may be able to help us decipher what we do not see with our ordinary senses. We can hope that someday soon we can advance through that veil.

Therefore the Cueva de los Tayos and its legacy are more alive than ever.

Appendices

Chronology of Events
Related to the Tayos Caves

1946 Petronio Jaramillo Abarca supposedly visits the cave in eastern Ecuador and sees the treasure of the metallic library. He writes about his experience ten years later in 1956.

1964 Jaramillo is interviewed by Alfredo Moebius, who introduces him to Andrés Fernández Salvador Zaldumbide, and Andrés introduces him to Juan Moricz and Pino Turolla.

1965 Moricz explores several Tayos caves, mainly in the Morona-Santiago region.

1968 The Mormon expedition with Julio Goyén Aguado and Avril Jesperson, representing the church of Latter-day Saints.

1969 The Moricz-CETURIS expedition, also called Táltosok Barlangja.

Second expeditions of CETURIS and the Ecuadorian army without Moricz. Moricz makes a notarized statement about his discoveries, but the statement will not be disclosed until 1974.

1972   Juan Moricz and his lawyer, Gerardo Peña Matheus, take Erich von Däniken to visit a cave outside of Cuenca.

1973   Because of the success of von Däniken's recently published *The Gold of the Gods,* notarized statements about the discoveries are made again, and Moricz and Peña Matheus attempt to sue von Däniken.

1974   Pino Turolla visits the caves and interviews Jaramillo for the first time. Another version of the story of the lost metallic library appears.

1975   Stanley Hall arrives from Scotland to meet Moricz and organize an expedition to the cave of the metallic library and to the Méndez petroglyphs.

1976   A joint scientific expedition between the UK and Ecuador with Stanley Hall. Neil Armstrong is an honorary participant in this event.

1978   Moricz introduces Hall to Andrés Fernández Salvador Zaldumbide.

1982   Moricz invites Hall to help him with the geological analysis of Cumbaratza.

      The death of Father Carlo Crespi.

1991   Moricz dies suddenly of a heart attack in February.

      Hall meets Petronio Jaramillo Abarca.

1996   Jaramillo adapts his version of the story of the treasure in the caves, which was originally published by Pino Turolla.

1998   Jaramillo is murdered by his son in suspicious circumstances in Esmeraldas.

1999 Julio Goyén Aguado dies in an accident during an archaeological expedition to the Mendoza Andes in Argentina.

2005 January 17: Hall publishes the location of the metallic library in a letter to the Ecuadorian ambassador in Britain.

2006– Alex E. Chionetti does several expeditions to the Tayos Caves
2007 in the Pastaza and Coangos River areas.

2008 Stanley Hall dies suddenly in Scotland, after being diagnosed with terminal cancer just two months before.

2009 Chionetti returns to the area of the Santiago River to visit the Tayos Caves that border Peru. He visits the mining zone of Cumbaratza and Nambija (Morona-Santiago).

2010 Chionetti discovers documents related to a metallic library lost in Bolivia but documented in books from the sixteenth century, among them the *Horca del Inca* in Copacabana.

Alex Chionetti gets a subsidiary of the History Channel to cover the topic and show images of the Tayos for a program called *Ancient Aliens*. The network shows the segment in November 2010 in an episode called "Underground Aliens."

Chronology of Alex Chionetti's Explorations

1978   A chapter in Chionetti's book *Mundos Paralelos* (Parallel worlds) discusses the subterranean, or the intraterrestrial.

1979   As a result of this book, Chionetti meets Julio Goyén Aguado.

1980   First trip to the Brujas Cavern, a cave that, according to Aguado, is interconnected, under the Andes, with the Tayos Cave in the Coangos River.

1981   Second expedition to the Brujas Cavern, and rediscovery of the Pueblo Plateau related to an ancient civilization.

   Trip to Peru, from which he tries to go to Guayaquil to meet Moricz and Father Crespi, but the border conflict interferes with his arrival.

   First expedition to the Marcahuasi Plateau in Peru.

1982   Organization of the Paititi Operation. Trained to survive in the jungle to do an expedition to the Tayos Caves, with the patronage of Hughes Aircraft and Coca-Cola, but the political situation in Argentina, Peru, and Ecuador forces the project to be abandoned.

1983   Living in Los Angeles, Chionetti meets an entrepreneur from Guayaquil, Enrique Inquieta, whom he visits to ask for funding for a documentary on the Tayos Caves. Inquieta doesn't help but offers him the position of editor of a weekly newspaper, *El Independiente,* which Chionetti will edit until 1985.

1987   Meets and rekindles his friendship with Aguado, who tells him of his experiences in the caves, confirming he saw the lost metallic library with Juan Moricz.

1997   In October when Chionetti is in Buenos Aires he plans an expedition with Aguado to the same Tayos Cave Aguado had explored with Moricz in 1968. The Discovery Channel is the possible producer and distributor of the documentary of the expedition, but it takes them months to come to a decision.

2000   Presents the project again to Discovery Science Channel.

2001   Second exploration of the Marcahuasi Plateau and documents.

2003   Fourth expedition to Marcahuasi, Peru. Excavations of the Infiernillo tunnel, with the intention to find a subterranean world and interconnecting elements with Tayos.

       Presents the Tayos project to National Geographic Television with the recommendation of the Smithsonian Institution and its National Museum of the American Indian.

2004   Presents the project to A&E Network's History Channel.

2005   Presents an exploration project about the study of the life of the tayos birds to National Geographic, but they depend on the television channels, and they decide the cave is not known or "important."

Presents the project to Frank Marshall (Kennedy/Marshall) by recommendation of Marvin Levy, Steven Spielberg's publicist.

The documentary of *The Mystery of the Tayos Caves* starts shooting, in coproduction with the Patagonian Express Company, Ecuavisa S.A., and Ecuavisa Internacional.

2006   Chionetti-Ecuavisa expedition to the Tayos Cave, Coangos, which is suspended due to several factors, one of them being the Shuar conflict with the Canadian mining companies. Also, a major from the Ecuadorian Air Force who was part of the team was so extremely cautious he stops Chionetti from fulfilling his destiny (the bridges over the Namangoza Gorge are closed).

First exploration of the Tayos Cave at the Pastaza River with the support of GITFA (Tactical Intervention Group of the Air Force) (November).

Second exploration of the Tayos Cave at the Pastaza River (December).

2007   Third expedition to the Tayos cave system, Coangos (March).

2008   Fourth expedition to the Tayos cave system, Santiago River (April).

2015   Presents and receives interest from Discovery Channel USA (decades after they were first interested) in a series about the Tayos Caves, though they recall Alex's potential participation due to another company pitching the same story at the same time, which supposedly was inspired by the author's official lecture at The Explorers Club in New York.

2016–   In association with a nature/travel Canadian filmmaker,
2017   Alex presents a new expedition with the participation of Neil Armstrong's descendants.

Companies such as A&E/History, Discovery Communications, National Geographic Television, and PBS all pass on Alex's ideas with excuses, mostly about the lack of evidence of the Metal Library. Later some will create programming about the Tayos, but without Alex's participation.

2019 Develops a new expedition with the assistance of two American speleologists to apply new techniques to study the biological and geological mysteries of the caves. Also, a new exploration of a secondary entrance is put in motion with the help of an Ecuadorian consultant for the tourism ministry.

Statement of Moricz's Lawyer Peña Matheus

Official statement of the lawyer Gerardo Peña Matheus about the Tayos, Moricz, and the first expedition for the official military and tourist discovery of 1969, as a response to the book The Mysteries of the Andes *by Robert Charroux.*

This French author, a pioneer on books about hidden treasures and lost civilizations, deformed several parts of the real story behind the Tayos, and also took advantage of the initial sensationalism of the story.

1. Afterwards, in the same complaint (a certified copy of it is attached) Mr. Juan Moricz requests the appointment of an "Ecuadorian commission, and he would only reveal to its members the *exact location of the several caves and caverns* that hold the artifacts he discovered."

2. I attach several copies of official memos that prove the Ministry of Finance of Ecuador received the aforementioned complaint, and they sent a copy of it to the General Procurement Office of the Nation, to the Ecuadorian House of Culture, and to the Ecuadorian Corporation of Tourism (CETURIS).

3. I attach a copy of statement N 1159 from July 15, 1969, sent by the Ecuadorian Corporation of Tourism to Dr. José María Velasco Ibarra, Constitutional President of the Republic. This statement proves CETURIS, as a consequence of the complaint by Mr. Juan Moricz, organized an official expedition which had the following objectives:

Find the caves and caverns that hold *the artifacts*.

Prove the existence of these artifacts.

Inform the truth of the discovery.

4. I attach a copy of the newspapers *El Telégrafo* from Guayaquil, and *El Comercio* from Quito, both editions from Sunday, September 18, 1969, as evidence that the story of the discovery of a "subterranean world in America" discovered by the "Moricz Expedition of 1969," organized by CETURIS was published in important newspapers with many photos. The following persons participated in this expedition:

MEMBERS OF THE MORICZ EXPEDITION OF 1969

JUAN MORICZ	Leader
GASTÓN FERNÁNDEZ	General Manager CETURIS
GERARDO PEÑA MATHEUS	Legal Advisor
LILIAN ICAZA	Coordinator
HERNÁN FERNÁNDEZ	Photographer
MARIO POLIT	Doctor
PEDRO LUNA	Assistant
JOSE ROJAS	Journalist

DEFENSE AND COMMUNICATIONS

CAPTAIN CARLOS GUERRERO GUERRÓN

SARGENT ORTIZ HERRERA: National Police Sargent

SENUSIANO AND SANCHEZ: Agents of the National Police

GUIDES

Army Corporal Segundo Guevara and Julio Cambizaca
The civilians Alfredo and Mario Punin

TRANSPORT

43 mules with their corresponding drivers

SCHEDULE

Departure from Guayaquil to Cuenca by car and truck, from Limón on mule to El Pescado, Tres Copales, La Esperanza, La Unión, where Corporal Julio Cambizaca was the commander. From here, they continued on a canoe to Puntilla, through the Santiago River, and its meeting with the Coangos River.

From here, they continued on foot to Jibaria to meet the witch Jukma from Coangos. Then on foot to the settlement of the "Moricz Expedition of 1969," which is in the part of Jibaria that belongs to Juajare.

5. I attach a copy of page 60 B of the international magazine *VISION*, available on the American continent, an edition from November 21, 1969, that serves as evidence that the news of the discovery of a "subterranean world" in America by the researcher Juan Moricz spread quickly.

6. I attach a copy of the article published in the magazine *VISTAZO*, an edition from December 1969, which proves, with plenty of photographic material, the discovery of a system of caves and caverns by the "Moricz Expedition of 1969."

7. I attach the original edition of the newspaper *El Telégrafo* from Guayaquil, from April 4, 1976, which announces the arrival of a British expedition to the mysterious caves and caverns discovered in 1969 by Mr. Juan Moricz.

There were some new explorers, among which we find Dr. Vagu Mijdahl, a member of the Danish Commission of Atomic Energy, who is mentioned in the book in relation to the Glozel plates and the thermoluminescence experiments. Moricz and I had the pleasure of meeting him during his stay in Guayaquil.

8. I attach the original clipping from the newspaper *El Universo,* from the city of Guayaquil, from Tuesday, August 3, 1976, which proves the famous North American astronaut Neil Armstrong (the first man on the moon) was a guest of the British expedition and visited the caves discovered seven years before by Mr. Juan Moricz.

9. I attach a copy of the map of the area around the caves and caverns investigated by the British team, for 1,500,000 pounds, which proves:

   a. The subterranean system is made up of several galleries and tunnels that lead to large caves and caverns.

   b. The galleries and tunnels cross over on different levels.

   c. The caves and caverns are located 610 feet deep under the surface of the earth.

   d. The location of the only entrance known to the subterranean system, which was made public by Mr. Juan Moricz in 1969, is located 3 degrees 6 minutes latitude south and 77 degrees 13 minutes longitude west from the Greenwich Meridian.

   e. The cartographic inspection of the subterranean area reached 3.04 miles.

   f. There are large subterranean chambers that are 984 ft. long × 262 ft. wide.

   g. There are passages longer than 984 ft. long.

   h. There are chimneys or ventilation shafts every couple of feet.

   i. The system continues under the Andes in areas that

still haven't been studied topographically, but their subterranean prolongation is evident.

10. I attach a copy of the magazine *VISTAZO* from the month of August 1976, which shows color photographs of weird tunnels, giant rocks, and constructions found 650 ft. deep in the Tayos Cave discovered in 1969 by Mr. Juan Moricz.

In summary, Mr. Juan Moricz is not an "adventurer," but a serious researcher, the wonderful network of galleries was not discovered in 1970, but in 1969, and I am not the "assistant" of adventurers, but a lawyer with a Ph.D. in Jurisprudence who intervened to verify the discovery, in my capacity as a Legal Advisor. There is no lack of evidence of the discovery; on the contrary, the evidence is abundant.

I am certain that once you examine the evidence I have sent about the discovery and "real existence of a fantastic network of galleries located 656 ft. deep that connect Ecuador with Peru," you will be able to rectify the audacious statement found on pages 101–02 of the edition of your book *The Mysteries of the Andes* that states, "In fact, neither the Swiss writer, nor Moricz, nor his assistant Gerardo Peña Matheus, *have provided the least bit of evidence* of their discoveries."

On page 102 of the Spanish edition of your book *The Mysteries of the Andes,* under subtitle "Mythomaniacs that hit the mark":

"Juan Moricz had said the Ecuadorian-Peruvian gallery had valuable objects, as well as the archives that prove the existence of an ancient and advanced civilization that disappeared before the Flood."

"Von Däniken was sure there was a hideout that held such things, but again, it was important to determine their location."

The Swiss writer stated in one of his books that in fact he had found the tunnel, and had seen golden statues of unknown animals, as well as many manuscripts printed in golden plates.

But—quoting the magazine *Nostradamus*—Juan Moricz denied this testimony, "and stated von Däniken never had access to the tunnel with the documents and artifacts of inestimable value."

The German magazine *STERN*, after contacting Moricz, also obtained evidence to prove the story of the writer was not true.

Stanley Hall's Letters

After several years of studying the particulars of the expeditions done by the explorers of the Tayos, I could observe the progress and setbacks they had. Through thousands of letters we have traveled through jungles, rivers, come and gone from cities and towns, risking the lives of those who have come with us, making our families worry for our lives, and risking their lives with our eccentric lifestyle.

I received many letters from Stanley Hall prior to his passing. As with all our characters, these contained contradictions, and many times when I tried to verify what he was saying, either in Ecuador or in the UK, I couldn't determine whether he was saying the truth or communicating through an idealistic or symbolic fashion in order to obscure the truth.

Stanley Hall's letters to the Ecuadorian authorities show his relentless efforts to make his dream come true. He wanted to prove the metallic library really did exist. For other important protagonists in the story, such as Gerardo Peña Matheus, the evidence of the subterranean world was the mysterious architecture of the main halls of the Coangos caves.

Among the letters sent before the expedition of 1976, we found many clues that would forecast what would happen in the upcoming legendary cycles of the caves.

Announcement to the Ecuadorian Congress: Congress 49, July 1997, Quito.

Mr. President, Ladies and Gentlemen:

My name is Stanley Hall from Edinburgh, Scotland. In 1976 I was the British Director of the great military-scientific expedition of the Tayos Caves, in the southwest of Ecuador. The honorary president and participant of that expedition was the professor-astronaut Neil Armstrong. More than a dozen universities and national and international institutions participated. I am an International Fellow of the Explorers Club of New York, "Honorary Member for Life" of the Federation of Shuar Nations and their international representative for the "Tayu Waa Project", which intends to put the Shuar and Achuar territories in Ecuador and Peru under the label of a World Heritage Site. An important condition of the Expedition of '76 was that there should be no attempts to find the legendary treasure that was supposed to be hidden within the enormous caves system, which goes from Venezuela to Argentina. However, I must admit I am fascinated by historical mysteries, and my background as a skeptical Scottish man keeps me safe. The only way I will believe in UFOs, in the Loch Ness Monster, or in hidden treasures is if someone brings them to my door.

There are treasures like those found with Tutankhamun, the Dead Sea Scrolls, the El-Amarna Letters in Egypt, the Ras Shamra Tablets in Lebanon, Henry Rawlinson's Sumero-Akkadian Inscriptions, and other findings that keep on changing our perception of ancient history. Then, why haven't we found any in America? It would be wonderful to find in this continent at least one metal plate with inscriptions. Finding a large metallic library and a large number of artifacts and tombs that seem to be sealed that represent a civilization that has been completely lost from history? Now that's what I am talking about!

All the discoverer needs is:

1. Protection for himself, the discovery, and his rights, in agreement with the Civil Code.
2. Publishing of the background manuscript, with illustrations to fully inform the public and the scientific world.
3. Preparation of the occupation expedition, for obvious reasons.
4. Acceptance that he (the discoverer) cannot disclose the exact location of the discovery until the background registry, the control committees, and the national and international components and agreements for the occupation expedition are defined.

In the following letter to the Ecuadorian ambassador in London, Hall introduces the first story and recontructs public testimony of Jaramillo, who wasn't known in Ecuador, only abroad, thanks to Turolla's book.

I found the discoverer, an Ecuadorian man from a good family, in October of 1992. His name is Petronio Jaramillo Abarca. We had several conversations where he described in detail the artifacts and historical archives he saw in the large gallery of the subterranean caves in eastern Ecuador.

The entrance is through a low tunnel under a river. After five years of collaboration I came to the unavoidable conclusion that my friend must have been speaking the truth, and I had to help him, as I felt greatly privileged he decided to put his trust in me. I didn't think it was possible he made up such a fantastic story; I felt he had really experienced it in the flesh.

Some of you might remember the speech given by the famous Richard Spruce in front of the Royal Geographical Society in London last century, where he talked of the famous document called "Valverde's Path," where he described the story of the fabulous hidden treasure of Atahualpa and Ruminyahui, supposedly located in the mountain region of the Llanganates in Ecuador. Researchers agreed the document was adulterated, and many explorers died in the search for this legendary Atahualpa treasure. This time the program was for an "Occupation" and not an "Exploration." The key words would be: good will, trust and organization.

Maybe Atahualpa's treasure and Petronio's Tahuantisuyu's treasure are identical; but, are they the same? Petronio and I decided the best moment to announce the discovery would be during this World Congress. And, as project coordinator, I had to assume this responsibility. The global plan included creating 4 control units:

1. A consulting committee of international and national ambassadors.
2. An international scientific, linguistic, and legal committee.
3. A liaison committee with UNESCO.
4. A scientific occupation expedition and international security.

The pertinent conversations with important embassies, with UNESCO, the Ministry of Foreign Relations and the Explorers Club have begun. Any initiative for international aid must be put in motion by the Ecuadorian authorities, and controlled under Ecuadorian law.

I can't explain how difficult these last few years have been, for the discoverer, for me, and for our families. It is now important to open the project to the public scope to avoid accusations, threats, and distortions, and to protect our families. James Bond and Indiana Jones don't exist in the real world. We are vulnerable because the treasures are never found by perfect explorers.

We will need your good will, your advice, and your scientific and linguistic help.

Now, I would like to give you some information that the discoverer has authorized me to share:

1. He decided to write his journal of the events before, during and after the discovery in a style he calls "parahistoric," to protect the integrity of the treasure and its historic truth.

2. The journal is called *The Last Secrets of Tahuantisuyu*. It will have 7 chapters, 300 pages of text and dozens of illustrations of facts that offer evidence, even if the text seems like a novel.

3. For the same reason that Neil Armstrong, the first man on the moon, is not the owner of a single square feet of it, Petronio Jaramillo Abarca, even if he has been inside the subterranean caves of the Tahuantisuyu treasure, does not believe he is the owner of this treasure. In both cases, Humanity is the sole owner.

4. The writing in the metallic library is very similar to modern short-hand, all the letters are written vertically, and there are no capital letters.

5. It shows all the geometric figures mankind could have invented, both for need or incidentally. These figures are shown in straight, vertical, and oblique lines. An important detail is that all these figures are split in two.

6. The metallic library is very large, and the books measure approximately 23.5 in × 19.5 in × 4 in (up to 6 in). Their average weight is 88 to 110 lb each.

7. There is a very curious colonial fact. In the pages of a book there is a paper written in ancient Spanish, signed by an officer called Juan Ruiz, from Francisco Pizarro's guard.

   The document was put there by a native, not by Ruiz. This paper says the Inca Huayna Capac had two legitimate sons, his heir Tankarhualpa and his second heir Huancarhualpa. Ruiz suspected his supposed uncle, Bartolomé Ruiz, arrived in the years 1523, 1525 and 1526 to the site where Tahuantisuyu's treasure was hidden, but since he did not agree to protect it, Tankarhualpa, the first heir did not disclose to him the exact location of the treasures.

I will be honored to receive the letters and summaries of the delegates and their institutions who are interested in the scientific side of this topic. Please contact me at the following address: Stanley Hall, Casilla de Correo Número 17-21-1324, Quito.

What was Hall's intention? Misinformation? Distraction? Because it is inconceivable that he made a 180-degree turn after he tried to help Moricz for so many years. He was skeptical with a scientific imagination and respected as having an advanced and expansive mind, not to mention grandiloquent. Why use the term *occupation*?

As my good friend Javier Stagnaro wrote: "Is he planning to stay and live in the cave? If Jaramillo was so sure and if they were such good friends, then why wasn't Jaramillo going with him and showing him the exact place; why was he beating around the bush? The caves are very large, but not so much that he can't pinpoint a specific place where he had a unique experience."

To continue with Stagnaro, I will quote an accurate observation he made. As a friend of Aguado and his assistant in his last years, Stagnaro lived this story up close:

From his youth, the Greco-Armenian mystic G. I. Gurdjieff had been obsessed with finding secret knowledge and teachings, and in one of his expeditions through the Middle Eastern deserts with a group called the "Seekers of Truth," he found a series of ancient engraved tablets. When he translated them, he realized they narrated a story he had listened to once before from his father: ancient knowledge could be preserved without changing its form.

Hall's contradictions have been flagrant. During our long chats, he used to tell me, "I never lied, there has never been, nor will there ever be room for lies." But yes, the facts were and are different. Aguado considered Hall's letters and appearances as bait to see who was interested.

Hall wrote me a letter to answer my questions before my final assault on the main Tayos Cave in the Coangos.

During his last years of life Hall knew he was too old to return to the Tayos region to fulfill his dream of finding the metallic library (and I believe his desire to find it was greater than the desire of the main protagonists). During this time he wrote me letters that showed he was a little hurt, because my letter had been the result of three months in Ecuador, interviewing many of the protagonists. There is no doubt a nationalistic fervor had gotten to me, making me choose my land, Latin America, and what had been considered official from the almost legendary rumors, from the British presence related to what was found, and not found, in the caves. Here is the original letter from Hall.

Friday, January 12, 2007

Subject: Re: MORITURI!!!!

Alex,

I am too far away to do more work and write reports; I have nothing more to add than what is already in my book, on the web site, and previous warnings of the few difficulties you are already going through. As you are having so many problems to handle your small team you are probably wondering how I organized and completed the giant expedition to the Tayos cave in 1976.

In a part of the e-mail you sent me personally you infer I was guilty of misinforming, of telling unverified stories, and a "bunch of bad intentions," this is why I want to address this first, so you can later choose what you want to believe. First, three key points:

1. Alleged British Pillage of the Coangos Cave

I am shocked someone as smart as you could believe this when the scientists of the expedition were of the highest repute—including Neil Armstrong—which was guarded and supervised by the Ecuadorian Special Forces. However, please see my page "Pre-history" on my website to see the recorded evidence of who moved the archaeological treasures of the site in the Tomb, declaring himself the discoverer, Father Pedro Porras. NOT THE BRITISH! I am forced to show this evidence because of the continuous ridiculous accusations and deformations by third parties who only have pieces of the information. The exhibit pieces at the Puce Museum. Talk to the director Patricio Moncayo and Dr. Guadalupe Dunnenberger. And please tell them I send them kind greetings!

2. Culture House

You forgot to add copies of the letters sent to Ulises and Wilma. Please send them to me with their e-mail addresses. For reasons similar to the ones I mentioned above, I have a small segment of Crespi's film—which I exchanged for the Tayos '76 film—and will upload [it] to my web page by the end of next week.

3. Letters to the ambassador of Ecuador in London, Mr. Cabezas

My initial letter was sent on December 6, 2004 after a phone conversation with the consul (Frank Bowen) who told me the ambassador wanted to write to me.

I sent a second letter to the ambassador on January 17, 2005, and this time I was careful enough to send a letter to the British

Office in London, who would have surely sent this letter to the British ambassador in Quito. Please look at the copies of these relevant letters attached to this e-mail!

- Petronio was constantly apologizing to me for lying to protect his "discovery." Yes, in that sense he was a pathological liar (Moricz had to act pretty much the same way). The details of the attack are dark.
- Surely Mario ([his son] from a second marriage, and who was single) was closer to his father more than [to] his mother Bertha, but Petronio and his eldest son from his first marriage were more alienated. Petronio died in Mario's arms.
- The guides, Luis Nivelo in Coangos and Bosco in Pastaza could be loyal to me, which would explain the ambivalence you noticed.
- In regards to Moricz, Goyén Aguado, and Grist, you know how I feel about them.
- I took two speleologist Australian scientists to the Coangos Cave (I have their professional reports and recommendations) when I was abandoned by the Spatz group, with the excuse that I was looking for photos for a book. I didn't even have a camera on me. They were tired and left me without food and water. I had to convince the Shuar who was with Nivelo not to throw them into the Santiago River.
- The border is marked by a line of markers or boundary stones, which are made of cement, and located mainly along the border of the Cóndor Range, just south of the Coangos cave.
- The Japanese (from the Expedition of 1993) jumped into the Coangos cave hoping to find treasures, with no scientific objectives. None of these stories compare to the British-Ecuadorian Expedition of '76.

You should choose your own path; but, looking at how far you've come, I can only tell you to step away from people who make you lose your time, or who could send you on useless searches as soon as possible.

I hope you take a good geologist with you, because otherwise you will make the classic and dangerous errors everyone has done before you.

I hope March 2007 brings you good luck.

ALL THE BEST,

STAN HALL

Bibliography

Aguirre, Guillermo. *Lirico y profundo: la vida de Julio Goyén Aguado.* LibrosEnRed, 2006.

Flornoy, Bertrand. *Jíbaro.* London: Elek, 1953.

Graeber, David and Marshal Sahlins. *On Kings.* London: Hau Books, 1989.

Hall, Stanley. *Savage Genesis.* Self-published in 2011. This book can be ordered through the Tayos Gold website.

———. *Tayos Gold: The Archives of Atlantis.* Kempton, Ill.: Adventures Unlimited, 2007.

Jesperon, Avril. Unpublished diary of his expedition.

Lourie, Peter. *Sweat of the Sun, Tears of the Moon.* New York: Atheneum, 1991.

Michell, John. *The View over Atlantis.* New York: Ballantine, 1977.

Molina, M. J. *Arqueología Ecuatoriana.* Quito, Ecuador: Abya-Yala, 1992.

Stagnaro, Javier. *Austeria: The Secret Doors to Agharta.* Buenos Aires: Edicion Privada del Autor, 2008.

Tayos Gold (website).

Turolla, Pino. *Beyond the Andes.* New York: Harper & Row, 1975.

Von Däniken, Erich. *The Gold of the Gods.* New York: Putnam, 1975.

Zagni, Marco. *El imperio amazónico.* Italy: Editorial MIR, 2002.

Index

Numbers in *italics* preceded by *pl.* indicate color insert plate numbers.

About the Author

Alex Chionetti was born in Buenos Aires, where he did his university studies. He is one of the most active and renowned South American explorers of recent years. In 2009, he received the Explorer's Medal from the Andean Explorer Foundation for his exploration in the Andes and Amazon jungles, especially for his expeditions to the cave systems of the Tayos.

An award-winning journalist, Chionetti also worked as a filmmaker and film and television distributor. He has been the editor of several newspapers and weekly and monthly journals in California, New Jersey, and New York. He has collaborated for two consecutive decades with the magazines *Más Allá de la Ciencia* (Beyond science) and *Año Cero* (Year zero), both from Spain.

He is the author of *Mundos Paralelos* (Parallel worlds; Editorial Cielosur, 1979). A new edition by Flying Disk Press was released in 2019.

He was an associate producer and creative consultant for the show *Ancient Aliens* on the History Channel (2009–11). Today he produces documentaries for international television broadcasters such as the SYFY channel, NBCUniversal, A&E, Telemundo, TVN 7 Perú, Ecuavisa S.A., and Canal 13 Argentina. He was also a consultant for Steven Spielberg's movie *Indiana Jones and the Kingdom of the Crystal Skull*.